AGS

PRACTICAL
GUIDE TO
*B*ETTER
ENGLISH

Level II

AGS®
American Guidance Service, Inc.
Circle Pines, Minnesota 55014-1796
1-800-328-2560

A NOTE TO STUDENTS

The *Practical Guide to Better English* teaches grammar, usage, mechanics, and writing skills. It is designed to help you become familiar with important elements of the English language and develop the written communication skills needed in school and in the workplace.

Completing the Lessons

Every lesson in this program is written so that you can complete it on your own. You can do this by following these steps:

1. Take a First Look

Read the lesson title. Ask yourself what you already know about this skill. If the title is "Punctuating Sentences," you might ask yourself: *What punctuation marks have I already learned about? Which of these marks are used at the end of a sentence?*

2. Learn the Rules

Look at the Handbook Guide numbers listed in the gray box at the beginning of the lesson. If there is a rule statement in the box, read it. Then find the numbered Guides in the Handbook, which starts on page 111. Read the rules and do the practice exercises. Check your answers by looking at the correct answers at the end of the numbered Guide or set of Guides. Then go back to the lesson page.

3. Think About the Topic

Scan the exercise sentences to find out what the topic is. Ask yourself: *What do I already know about this subject?* If you're working with a partner or group, share some facts about the topic. Reviewing what you already know can help you get more out of what you read.

4. Complete the Lesson

Many lessons have two parts. Read the directions for the first part and think about what you're being asked to do. Ask for help if you don't understand the directions. Then complete the exercise. Use the Handbook Guide to help you if you are uncertain about an answer. Then follow the same steps for Part II. Some lessons have a vocabulary activity at the bottom of the page. If there is a vocabulary activity, complete it last.

5. Check Your Answers

With your group or class, identify the correct answer for each item. If you have an Answer Key, check your work yourself. The Perfect Score for each lesson is given at the top of the page. Count your correct answers and write your score in the blank at the top of the page. Then record your score on the chart on page 176.

6. Sum It Up

Think about what you learned in the lesson. You might want to write the Handbook Guide rule used in the lesson in your own words. Think about how you can use this skill when you write or speak.

Reviewing What You've Learned

The last lesson in every unit gives you a chance to review the skills in that unit. The unit review lesson is not a test. It's there to help you recall what you've learned and put that new knowledge to work. The Handbook Guides are listed with each item, so you can check a rule if you need to before you complete the item.

Printed in the United States of America
ISBN 0-7854-1789-3
Product Number 93071
A 0 9 8 7 6 5 4 3 2

CONTENTS

LESSON I
Recognizing Sentences

Handbook Guide 1a

A sentence is a group of words that expresses a complete thought.

PART I Write the word *yes* before each group of words that is a sentence. Write the word *no* before each group of words that needs something else to complete the thought. (Score: 10)

Examples:

_____*yes*_____ Downhill skiing is a demanding event.

_____*no*_____ Speeds of more than 65 miles per hour.

_____ 1. Picabo Street began her skiing career at the age of five.

_____ 2. She joined the U.S. National Ski Team before her sixteenth birthday.

_____ 3. A silver medal at the 1994 Winter Olympics in Lillehammer, Norway.

_____ 4. During the 1995 World Cup season she won six downhill races.

_____ 5. First American woman to win a World Cup downhill championship.

_____ 6. Voted the Sportswoman of the Year by the United States Olympic Committee.

_____ 7. She tore a ligament in her knee while training in December of 1996.

_____ 8. More than a year to recover from that injury.

_____ 9. In the 1998 Winter Olympics Picabo Street won another gold medal.

_____ 10. In a different event, the women's super-G!

PART II Add words to the following word groups to make sentences. (Score: 6—3 for each sentence)

Example:

(physical and mental preparation)

Downhill skiing requires physical and mental preparation.

11. (a very steep slope) _____

_____

12. (the best skiers in the world) _____

_____

Name _____   Perfect Score 33   My Score _____

LESSON 2
Punctuating Sentence Endings

Handbook Guides 1c–e

Place a period at the end of a statement.
Place a question mark at the end of a
question. Place an exclamation point at
the end of an exclamatory sentence.

PART I   Place the appropriate punctuation mark at the end of each sentence below. If the sentence is a statement, write *S* in the blank before the sentence; if it is a question, write *Q*; and if it is an exclamatory sentence, write *E*. (Score: 24)

Examples:

_____*Q*_____   Who is Chick Corea?

_____*S*_____   He is a pianist and a composer.

_____*E*_____   What an amazing sense of rhythm he has!

_____   1. Chick Corea is a very inventive jazz pianist

_____   2. Doesn't he play electronic instruments on many recordings

_____   3. What a solid beat that song has

_____   4. Who is the bass player

_____   5. His name is Stanley Clarke

_____   6. What a fine musician he is

_____   7. Isn't jazz harder to play than rock

_____   8. Have you heard Chick Corea's record of Latin music

_____   9. Yes, but I prefer his piano solos

_____   10. How peaceful they make me feel

_____   11. My favorite album of his is *Three Quartets*

_____   12. Doesn't he include tributes to John Coltrane and Duke Ellington on this recording

PART II   On the lines below, write a statement, a question, and an exclamation about the kind of music you like. (Score: 9—3 for each sentence)

13. _____

14. _____

15. _____

LESSON 3
Writing Names

Handbook Guide 2b

Begin the name of a person, a place, or a company with a capital letter.

PART I   In the following sentences, underline the uncapitalized words that should begin with a capital letter. (Score: 45)

Examples:

Many TV talk shows are filmed in <u>new</u> <u>york</u> <u>city</u>.

One of <u>america</u>'s favorite talk show hosts is <u>rosie</u> o'Donnell.

1. Rosie o'Donnell grew up in commack, new york.

2. Her father had come to the united states from ireland.

3. Rosie's mother died of cancer when rosie was ten.

4. After that, rosie helped take care of other family members, including her grandmother.

5. Rosie played sports in high school, and she also loved watching barbra streisand and bette midler on TV.

6. Rosie o'Donnell got her start as a performer when she was sixteen.

7. She did stand-up comedy in clubs on long island.

8. O'Donnell attended dickinson college and boston university.

9. In the early 1990s she appeared in movies with tom hanks and meg ryan.

10. Today o'Donnell hosts a talk show that is filmed in rockefeller center.

11. The studio is at fiftieth street and sixth avenue in manhattan.

12. Rosie treats guests with respect, as did mike douglas, merv griffin, and other talk show hosts.

13. She says she enjoys talking with authors such as anne rice and pat conroy.

14. In addition to performing, o'Donnell cares for her son, parker jaren, and her daughter, chelsea belle.

PART II   In the blank spaces, write names for the following items. (Score: 6)

Example:

a county   _____*Hennepin County*_____

15. a city _____

16. a country _____

17. a river _____

18. a high school _____

19. a sports team _____

20. an ocean _____

LESSON 4
Using Capital Letters

> **Handbook Guides 2a, 2b, 3, 4**
>
> **Capitalize an initial used in place of a name. Capitalize titles used before a name. Place a period after a title if it is abbreviated.**

In the sentences below underline each word that should begin with a capital letter. (Score: 75)

Richmond, Oregon

1. richmond, oregon, is now a ghost town.

2. richmond is southeast of the john day river.

3. many ghost towns in oregon, california, nevada, and utah were once mining towns.

4. the town of richmond was built by farmers and ranchers, however.

5. mr. caleb n. thornburg was one of the founders of richmond.

6. some other founders were the gilburgs, the donnellys, and the walterses.

7. a meeting was held to plan oregon's newest town.

8. the year was 1889; oregon had been part of the united states for thirty years.

9. r. n. donnelly and william walters had a loud argument about where the school should be built.

10. mr. donnelly called mr. walters "jeff davis" because he thought walters was rebellious.

11. perhaps you know that jefferson davis was the leader of the confederate states of america.

12. then donnelly said that they might as well call the town richmond.

13. richmond, virginia, was the capital of the confederate states of america.

14. later mr. donnelly donated three acres of land for the school.

15. people remembered what he had said, and they called the town richmond.

16. a store and the richmond methodist church were soon built.

17. the wheeler county pioneers, a club, had a rip-roaring celebration in richmond in 1901.

18. many small towns like richmond began to die when the automobile became popular.

19. people living near richmond began to drive to larger towns such as prineville.

20. one by one the buildings of richmond were abandoned.

Connecting Meanings

Draw a line from each word in row 1 to its meaning in row 2. Then write a sentence using each word in row 1.

Row 1	luminous	ominous	ludicrous
Row 2	menacing	ridiculous	shining

LESSON 5
Using Commas

Handbook Guides 7d, 11, 12, 13a

In sentences, use commas to separate parts of an address, the name of the person being addressed, introductory words such as *yes* or *no*, and words in a series.

PART I   In the following sentences, place commas where they are needed. (Score: 19)

Rodeo Thrills

1.   Why are all those people wearing boots bolo ties and Stetson hats?

2.   Tomorrow is the first day of the Calgary Stampede Cheryl.

3.   Men women and children dress in western styles during the Stampede.

4.   Is the Calgary Stampede a rodeo Jeannie?

5.   Yes it's one of the largest in North America.

6.   Is the Calgary Stampede more exciting than the rodeo in Cheyenne Wyoming?

7.   I think all of them are exciting Cheryl.

8.   My cousin from Llano Texas hopes to become a rodeo rider.

9.   I've seen her practice roping bulldogging and trick riding.

10.   She's usually tired dusty and bruised afterward.

11.   Cheryl is there any reason why we shouldn't join in the square dance?

12.   No not unless your toes are tender.

13.   Maybe we should grab some flapjacks bacon and coffee instead.

PART II   Rewrite the following sentences, placing commas where they are needed. (Score: 6)

14.   We're going to a rodeo in New York City New York. _____

_____

15.   Mac have you ever watched the event called saddle bronc riding? _____

_____

16.   A saddle a halter and one rein are placed on a bronco. _____

_____

17.   The rider tries to stay on that horse while it jumps plunges and bucks. _____

_____

Name_____ Perfect Score 19 My Score _____

LESSON 6
Using Is *and* Are, Was *and* Were

> **Handbook Guides 19, 20**
>
> Use *is* and *was* when you speak of one person or thing. Use *are* and *were* when you speak of more than one person or thing. Always use *are* and *were* with you, whether it refers to one person or to more than one.

PART I Draw a line under the appropriate word in parentheses. (Score: 15)

1. The Hawaiian goose (is, are) Hawaii's state bird.

2. In the Hawaiian language this bird (is, are) called the *néné.*

3. Once these birds (was, were) numerous on the Hawaiian islands.

4. But by 1780 they (was, were) being killed in great numbers.

5. Hawaii (was, were) then a port of call for whaling ships.

6. These geese (was, were) killed, salted, and packed aboard the ships.

7. Hunting (was, were) not the only reason the geese became scarce.

8. The eggs (was, were) taken from their nests.

9. Forests where they lived (was, were) cut down.

10. Animals brought to Hawaii by settlers (was, were) harmful, too.

11. A nest built on the ground (was, were) likely to be trampled by cows or horses.

12. By 1900 very few Hawaiian geese (was, were) still alive.

13. Herbert C. Shipman (was, were) worried that the néné would become extinct.

14. A néné colony (was, were) started by him at his home in Keaau.

15. Three birds from this colony (was, were) sent to England in 1951.

PART II Fill each blank with the appropriate form in parentheses. (Score: 4)

16. (was, were) By 1958 there _____ seventy-three geese in that flock.

17. (was, were) Some of these _____ then returned to wild areas in Hawaii.

18. (is, are) Hawaiian geese _____ now protected by law.

19. (is, are) Apparently the Hawaiian goose _____ now in much less danger of becoming extinct.

Name That Job _____

Decide what occupation the person who uses these things probably has. Then write a paragraph telling how each item is used.

light meter   tripod   flash   lens   film

LESSON 7
Writing Abbreviations

PART I   Write the abbreviation for each of the following words. If a word cannot be abbreviated, write the full word on the line. (Score: 18)

1. Sunday _____   7. Monday _____   13. Tuesday _____

2. Wednesday _____   8. Thursday _____   14. Friday _____

3. Saturday _____   9. January _____   15. February _____

4. March _____   10. April _____   16. May _____

5. July _____   11. August _____   17. September _____

6. October _____   12. November _____   18. December _____

PART II   Rewrite the following addresses. Use abbreviations for social, academic, and professional titles and for other words that it is correct to abbreviate. (Score: 12–1 for each line)

Example:

Mister Ed Hamilton   *Mr. Ed Hamilton* _____

1401 Northeast Polk Boulevard   *1401 NE Polk Blvd.* _____

Tyler, Texas 75701   *Tyler, TX 75701* _____

19.   Doctor Betty Klimkowski   _____
      1620 West Main Street   _____
      Freeport, New York 11520   _____

20.   Mister Arturo Ramirez   _____
      602 Buena Vista Avenue   _____
      Tucson, Arizona 85700   _____

21.   Miss Linda Coelho   _____
      1121 Northwest 20th Street   _____
      Richmond, Virginia 23200   _____

22.   Judge Homer Yee   _____
      1548 12th Avenue   _____
      San Francisco, California 94122   _____

Name_____   Perfect Score 38 My Score _____

LESSON 8
Punctuating Sentences

PART I Place commas and end punctuation in the sentences below. (Score: 27)

A TV News Reporter

1. Does Christine still want to be a reporter Sally

2. Yes Sam she has been hired by a television station

3. Will I see her on the six o'clock news tonight

4. Yes she will be covering the mayor's speech

5. How lucky she is to have such a great job

6. Sam Christine didn't get her job by being lucky

7. She studied speech and journalism at Louisiana State University

8. Christine has learned to speak write and think clearly

9. She admires the work of Charlayne Hunter-Gault Cokie Roberts and Diane Sawyer

10. Don't you think they are talented intelligent and well spoken

11. Perhaps Christine will become a reporter for a national network

12. No Christine says that she prefers to live here

13. New Orleans Louisiana is an exciting place to live

PART II Rewrite the sentences below, adding punctuation. (Score: 11)

14. Christine speaks in a strong clear pleasant voice _____

    _____

15. Has she interviewed anyone famous _____

    _____

16. Yes Sam she talked with our governor last week _____

    _____

17. How I wish I had a job like hers _____

    _____

18. Maybe you should take courses in journalism political science and speech _____

    _____

LESSON 9
Identifying Sentences

In each of the following paragraphs there are four sentences. Identify the sentences and put the proper punctuation at the end of each sentence. Draw a line under each word that begins a new sentence and should be capitalized. (Score: 20—1 for each sentence)

Granville T. Woods

      Granville T. Woods was an inventor he created many important electrical devices several of these have helped Americans live happier, safer lives some people have compared Woods to Thomas Edison

      Woods was born in 1856 in Columbus, Ohio he had to leave school when he was ten years old he then worked at several factory jobs he always paid close attention to how the factory machines worked

      Woods first became interested in electricity when he was sixteen at that time electricity was just beginning to be used he read many books about electricity later, in 1881, he opened a factory that made electrical equipment

      Woods invented two important things in 1884 the first item was an improved furnace to produce steam heat the second item was a telephone transmitter the transmitter was something like the voice transmitters in today's telephones

      In later years Woods invented a system that let the engineer on a moving train talk with people in railroad stations this invention made travel by train much safer he also invented several electric trolley systems he is the inventor of the third rail, which many rapid transit systems use today.

Word Whiz _____

Use the clues on the left to help you complete the words on the right. Use a dictionary for spelling help.

part of a turkey's digestive system	__ __ z z a r d
large bird that is a scavenger	__ __ __ z z a r d
big snowstorm	__ __ __ z z a r d

Name_____

LESSON 10
Writing a Descriptive Paragraph

Read a Descriptive Paragraph

Handbook Guide 28

The purpose of a descriptive paragraph is to inform readers about what a person, place, thing, or event is like. To write a descriptive paragraph, use a topic sentence, give supporting details in the body of the paragraph, and use colorful language.

When you write to tell what a person, place, thing, or event is like, you are creating a **description**. A well-written description can help your readers picture what you saw. Here are some guidelines for writing an effective descriptive paragraph:

- Begin your paragraph with a **topic sentence** that lets the reader know what you will be describing.

- In the rest of the paragraph, give several **supporting details** that tell more about what you are describing.

- Try to use **colorful words and phrases** that appeal to the five senses: sight, hearing, taste, smell, touch.

- Let the reader know **how you feel** about what you're describing.

Read this example of a descriptive paragraph:

A Treasured Possession

My favorite possession is the guitar my grandfather kindly willed to me when he died. It's not shiny, new, flashy, or expensive. It is old and worn, but it has a beauty new things just don't have. This guitar is forty years old. Its wood has darkened into a nut-brown color. Many years of playing have given it a deep, rich sound. If you softly run your finger along the smooth wood, you can feel small nicks on the finish from many years of use. My grandfather's guitar smells of old wood and polish, a pleasant smell something like cedar. I can only play a few simple chords, the ones my grandfather patiently taught me. Whenever I pick up the guitar to play it, I am reminded of him. If I ever do become a famous guitar player and have loads of money to spend, I still will never replace that old guitar.

Complete these items about the descriptive paragraph above.

1. What is the topic of this paragraph?_____

2. Which sentence tells the reader what will be described? Underline it.

3. Where in the paragraph does this sentence appear? _____

4. The author has used many details to give readers a feeling for what his guitar is like. Reread the paragraph. Look for details that appeal to the five senses: sight, hearing, taste, touch, and smell. On the lines, write some details the author has used.

   sight_____

smell   _____

sound   _____

5.   How does the author seem to feel about the guitar? How can you tell?

_____

_____

6.   Underline the adjectives the writer has used.

Write a Descriptive Paragraph

Think of a possession you value a lot. It could be a favorite piece of clothing, a musical instrument, or something someone gave you. Write a descriptive paragraph about that possession. You can use the paragraph on page 14 as a model.

1.   Plan

Use this space to plan your descriptive paragraph. In the middle of the web, write the name of the possession you want to write about. In the outside circles, list some details that appeal to the five senses.

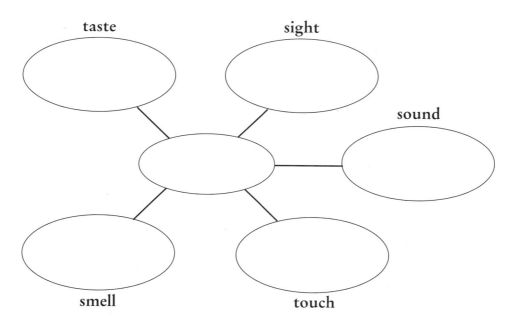

2.   Write

Write your description on another piece of paper. Use your notes in the web to guide you.

3.   Reread and Correct

Now reread your paragraph. Look for mistakes in spelling. Look up any words you're not sure of. Also make sure that your paragraph has a topic sentence. Then make corrections. If you want, you can make a clean copy of your corrected paragraph.

Name_____   Perfect Score 40   My Score _____

LESSON II
Unit I Review

1. Add words and punctuation to the following word groups to make sentences. Use capital letters where needed. (Score: 2)

    Handbook Guides 1, 2a

    (has a ticket to Puerto Rico) _____

    _____

    (to the airport on Saturday) _____

    _____

2. Rewrite the sentences below, using appropriate punctuation marks and capital letters. (Score: 28)

    Handbook Guides 1b–e, 2b, 7d, 11, 12, 13a

    nikki does juan live in portland maine _____

    _____

    no juliette he lives near faneuil hall in boston massachusetts _____

    _____

    three great people of boston were john adams sam adams and abigail adams _____

    _____

3. In the first column write an example for the words in parentheses. In the second column write the abbreviation of the name in the first column. For the state, write the postal code abbreviation. (Score: 6)

    Handbook Guides 2b–d, 5, 6, 7c

    (a day of the week)   _____   _____

    (a month)   _____   _____

    (a state)   _____   _____

4. On the lines below, write sentences using the words in parentheses. (Score: 4)

    Handbook Guides 19, 20

    (is) _____

    (are) _____

    (was) _____

    (were) _____

Name_____ Perfect Score 6   My Score _____

LESSON 12
Identifying Paragraph Topics

> **Handbook Guide 28a**
>
> **The beginning sentence of a paragraph should introduce the topic that is being discussed.**

Read these three paragraphs. Then answer the questions below. (Score: 6)

A.   The giant panda is an unusual animal. It is large and heavy and looks somewhat like a bear. It is not a bear, however. It is a relative of the raccoon. The giant panda's home is the mountains of southwestern China. The panda's favorite foods are bamboo shoots and bamboo roots. It is a very shy animal. Few humans have ever seen a giant panda in the wild.

B.   Firefighters are very busy even when they aren't fighting fires. They talk to people about fire safety. They inspect apartments, offices, and factories for fire hazards. They keep their trucks and equipment in good condition. Sometimes they rescue people from dangerous situations. Many firefighters also answer calls for first aid.

C.   Our town is in danger of being flooded. We have had a long, hard winter. There is a record amount of snow on the ground. As the snow melts, the river will swell. We have placed sandbags along the riverbank near our town. Unless the snow melts slowly, however, the strong flow of water will wash the sandbags away and the river will overflow its banks.

1.   What is the topic of paragraph A? _____

2.   What does the paragraph tell about this topic? _____

3.   What is the topic of paragraph B? _____

4.   What does the paragraph tell about this topic? _____

5.   What is the topic of paragraph C? _____

6.   What does the paragraph tell about this topic? _____

Name_____   Perfect Score 25   My Score _____

LESSON 13
Writing Paragraphs

Handbook Guide 28

A paragraph is a group of sentences that tells about one topic, or subject.

Study the Handbook section that tells how to write a paragraph. Then use the details below to write your own paragraph on the lines below. (Score: 25)

gorillas—look fierce but aren't   live in family units

largest of all apes   foods: fruit, bark, leaves

450 pounds (male)   only attack when threatened

200 pounds (female)

intelligent and powerful but shy

_____

_____

_____

_____

_____

_____

_____

_____

_____

_____

_____

_____

Check your paragraph. Does the first sentence give the topic of the paragraph? Do the other sentences all tell about the topic?

LESSON 14
Punctuating Quotations

Handbook Guides 1b–e, 2h, 9

Put quotation marks around the exact words of a speaker. Capitalize the first word of a quotation. Place the punctuation mark at the end of a quotation inside the quotation mark.

PART I Place quotation marks and commas where they are needed. Underline each word that should begin with a capital letter. (Score: 36)

Example:

Zack said my aunt has just become a coal miner.

Zack said, "my aunt has just become a coal miner."

1. Anita said my uncle is a miner, too.

2. he doesn't mine coal, though she continued.

3. what kind of miner is your uncle? asked Judy.

4. he works in a salt mine in Texas Anita replied.

5. Zack said I thought salt was found only in seawater.

6. salt comes from mines, wells, the sea, and even lakes said Anita.

7. my uncle likes working in a salt mine she continued.

8. his mine is in an underground mountain of rock salt she explained.

9. Judy said I think that's called a salt dome.

10. can you tell me how salt is mined? asked Zack.

PART II Rewrite the quotations below, adding all necessary punctuation marks. (Score: 16–4 for each sentence)

11. Anita said The miners cut and drill deep into a wall of salt _____

_____

12. Then they set off an explosive charge she continued _____

_____

13. The explosion makes the wall of salt collapse, doesn't it asked Judy _____

_____

14. Anita said Yes, and then the salt is loaded onto a moving belt _____

_____

Synonym Watch _____

Circle the word in the second row that is a synonym for a word in the first row. Then draw a line to connect it to its synonym. Write a sentence in which you can use either word.

| **Row 1** | meddle | medal | metal |
| **Row 2** | interpret | interfere | internal |

LESSON 15
Punctuating Direct and Indirect Quotations

Handbook Guide 9

A direct quotation gives the exact words of a speaker and is enclosed in quotation marks. An indirect quotation does not give the exact words of a speaker and is not enclosed in quotation marks.

Examples: Mr. Pritchard asked, "Why are we having a meeting?" (direct quotation)

Mr. Pritchard asked why we were having a meeting. (indirect quotation)

PART I   Punctuate the following direct and indirect quotations. Add necessary quotation marks, commas, and other punctuation marks. (Score: 33)

1. We're going to talk about conserving energy said Ms. Nakai

2. Mrs. Simic said that all people should lower their thermostat settings

3. We already keep ours at 65 degrees during the day said Mrs. Jones

4. Ms. Nakai then asked her how she keeps herself warm

5. I usually wear a turtleneck and a sweater Mrs. Jones answered

6. Our thermostat is set at 55 degrees during the night said Miss Mah

7. Ms. Nakai explained that she turns off the heat in her home at night

8. You must freeze exclaimed Mrs. Simic

9. We close off the rooms we're not using said Mrs. Jones

10. Mrs. Simic asked whether Mrs. Jones also closed the heat registers in those rooms

11. Yes, Mrs. Simic, I do answered Mrs. Jones

PART II   Rewrite the following indirect quotations as direct quotations. Add all necessary punctuation and capitalization. (Score: 12—4 for each sentence)

12. Mr. Pritchard said that everyone should do less driving. _____

_____

13. Mrs. Simic said that she bought a bicycle last week. _____

_____

14. She explained that riding a bicycle helps conserve energy. _____

_____

Optional Exercise: Rewrite the sentences in Part I, changing direct quotations to indirect quotations and changing indirect quotations to direct quotations.

LESSON 16
Choosing Standard Verb Forms—
Teach *and* Learn, May *and* Can

Handbook Guides 33, 35

To teach means "to instruct someone else."
To learn means "to receive instruction."
Use *may* to ask or give permission to do
something. Use *can* to show that someone
is able to do something.

PART I Draw a line under the appropriate word in
parentheses. (Score: 6)

Examples: When did you (teach, <u>learn</u>) to make maple sugar biscuits?

A friend from Vermont (<u>taught</u>, learned) me last summer.

1.   My friend first (taught, learned) me how to chop hickory nuts.

2.   I (taught, learned) why the dry ingredients must be sifted twice.

3.   I had already been (taught, learned) how to whip heavy cream.

4.   My friend also (taught, learned) me how to fold and roll biscuit dough.

5.   Every cook must (teach, learn) when to preheat an oven.

6.   No one had to (teach, learn) me how to eat maple sugar biscuits.

PART II Fill the blanks with the appropriate word, *may* or *can*. (Score: 9)

Examples: ____*May*____ I bring some gingerbread to the party?

You ____*may*____ bring it if you ____*can*____ be here by 7:30.

7.   _____ I try a piece of your banana nut bread?

8.   I _____ help you cut vegetables for the salad.

9.   Eddie says that I _____ serve myself a bowl of chili.

10. See whether you _____ follow the recipe for molasses butter.

11. Eddie, you _____ cut the corn bread into squares.

12. _____ you pass the pickled jalapeño peppers?

13. _____ I ask why we have so much food here?

14. I _____ see why nobody dances at your parties.

15. No, Eddie, you _____ not have a doggy bag.

Connecting Meanings _____

Draw a line from each word in row 1 to its meaning in row 2. Then write a sentence using
each word in row 1.

Row 1	culinary	culminate	cultivate
Row 2	grow	having to do with cooking	reach the highest point

Name_____   Perfect Score 36   My Score _____

LESSON 17
Writing Contractions

> **Handbook Guides 14, 20**
> **Use an apostrophe to show where one or more letters are left out.**

PART I   Write the contractions of the following words. (Score 14)

Example: do not   _____*don't*_____

1.	is not	_____	8.	have not	_____
2.	are not	_____	9.	had not	_____
3.	was not	_____	10.	cannot	_____
4.	were not	_____	11.	will not	_____
5.	does not	_____	12.	should not	_____
6.	did not	_____	13.	would not	_____
7.	has not	_____	14.	could not	_____

PART II   Draw a line under the appropriate words in parentheses. At the end of each sentence write the contraction of the words you have underlined. (Score: 22)

15.   The Broadway musical *The Lion King* (is not, are not) just a weak copy   _____
of the movie.

16.   This show (do not, does not) look anything like most musicals.   _____

17.   Julie Taymor (is not, are not) just a director, she is also a costume   _____
designer for her shows.

18.   When she planned the musical version of *The Lion King*, she (was not,   _____
were not) afraid to try new ideas.

19.   Many of the animal costumes (is not, are not) suits; they are puppets.   _____

20.   The actors (does not, do not) hide while operating the puppets.   _____

21.   Most audiences (has not, have not) seen actors carrying puppets on stage.   _____

22.   This complex show (was not, were not) easy to put together.   _____

23.   In rehearsals some special effects (was not, were not) working properly.   _____

24.   Despite the difficulties, Ms. Taymor (did not, do not) become   _____
discouraged.

25.   In my opinion, the musical version of *The Lion King* (would not,   _____
should not) be nearly as interesting without the puppets.

Optional Exercise: Write sentences using each of the contractions in Part I.

LESSON 18
Avoiding Double Negatives

Handbook Guide 39

No, not, nobody, none, never, and *hardly* are negative words. Use only one negative word to express a negative idea.

Rewrite the following sentences, correcting the double negatives. (Score: 10)

Example: I don't have no hubcaps on my car. *(don't* and *no* make a double negative)
I don't have any hubcaps on my car. (or) I have no hubcaps on my car.

1. We can't drive this old car no more. _____
   _____

2. We don't have hardly enough money to buy a better one. _____
   _____

3. Maybe we can afford a used car that doesn't have no extras. _____
   _____

4. There aren't no bargains on some car lots. _____
   _____

5. Nobody has never made a bad deal at Quality Motors. _____
   _____

6. They don't have nothing but good cars at fair prices. _____
   _____

7. A few dents don't bother me none. _____
   _____

8. We don't want no car without no radio, though. _____
   _____

9. Let's not waste no more time talking. _____
   _____

10. I hope our old car doesn't lose no more oil on the way to the lot. _____
    _____

Name_____   Perfect Score 20   My Score _____

LESSON 19
Choosing Standard Verb Forms

Handbook Guide 21

Use helping verbs with such verbs as *driven, known, seen,* and *taken.* Do not use helping verbs with such verbs as *broke, did, rode, went,* and *wrote.*

PART I   In each blank write the appropriate verb in parentheses. (Score: 13)

1. (saw, seen) Have you ever _____ a horse race?

2. (saw, seen) The Kentucky Derby can be _____ on TV every year.

3. (saw, seen) Our group _____ the race last year.

4. (knew, known) It is _____ as "The Run for the Roses."

5. (went, gone) We had _____ to Louisville to see it.

6. (took, taken) It _____ place on the first Saturday in May.

7. (wrote, written) Our sponsor had _____ for tickets in March.

8. (drove, driven) Some of the group had _____ to Louisville.

9. (rode, ridden) The rest of us _____ the bus.

10. (saw, seen) We had never _____ such beautiful horses.

11. (rode, ridden) They are _____ by some of the world's best jockeys.

12. (drove, driven) Many people _____ hundreds of miles to see the race.

13. (went, gone) After the race was over, we _____ home.

PART II   If a sentence below has an inappropriate verb form, rewrite the sentence correctly on the line. If a sentence is correct, copy it on the line. (Score: 7)

14. That horse has broke the track record. _____

15. The trainer done her work well. _____

16. Now she has gone to the stables. _____

17. A photographer gone with her. _____

18. She has already took some pictures of the horse. _____

19. The owner ridden away in a big limo. _____

20. He said, "I knew I had a winner!" _____

LESSON 20
More Verb Forms

PART I   Draw a line under the appropriate verb form in parentheses. (Score: 16)

1. Few pitchers have (threw, thrown) as hard or as accurately as Lefty Gomez.

2. Gomez (come, came) to the New York Yankees in 1930.

3. Much has been (wrote, written) about the stars of early Yankee teams.

4. The Yankee hitters were (knew, known) as "The Window Breakers."

5. Babe Ruth, Lou Gehrig, and Tony Lazzeri (did, done) much of the damage.

6. The Yankees (went, gone) all the way to the World Series in 1932.

7. The Chicago Cubs (come, came) into the series hungry for victory.

8. Red Ruffing (come, came) through for the Yanks with a victory in the opener.

9. Gomez (threw, thrown) nothing but strikes in the second game.

10. But that series has (come, came) to be remembered for one thing in particular.

11. In the third game Babe Ruth (come, came) to the plate.

12. He (did, done) something daring by pointing with his bat to the center field stands.

13. The next pitch was (threw, thrown) hard, and Ruth swung hard.

14. Everyone (saw, seen) Ruth's homer land right where he had pointed.

15. Many stories have been (wrote, written) about how Babe Ruth called his shot.

16. The Yankees (gone, went) on to sweep the series.

PART II   Write a short sentence on each line below, using the verb in parentheses. Helping verbs will be needed in some sentences. (Score: 8)

17. (became) _____

18. (broken)_____

19. (begun) _____

20. (sank)_____

21. (gave) _____

22. (drawn) _____

23. (grew) _____

24. (flown) _____

Name_____

LESSON 21
Writing a Personal Narrative

Read a Personal Narrative

When you write to tell about an experience in your life, you create a **personal narrative**. Writing about personal experiences can help you preserve and share important moments. Here are some guidelines for writing an effective personal narrative:

- Tell about events from **the first-person point of view**: use the pronouns *I, me, mine,* and *my.*
- Make sure your narrative has a **beginning**, a **middle**, and an **end**.
- Be sure to tell **where** and **when** the events happened.
- Help the reader understand **the order in which the events took place** by using words such as *first, next, then,* and *finally.*
- Describe your feelings as well as your actions. Use colorful adjectives and expressive adverbs.

Read this example of a personal narrative:

A Flight I'd Rather Forget

I had always wanted to take a ride in a small plane. I wanted to feel the freedom that birds feel as they fly through the open sky. On my fourteenth birthday, my chance finally came. My uncle Jack arranged a flight in a friend's small plane as a gift. When we got to the airfield, I saw a sleek, gorgeous red-and-white plane and started to run toward it. "Cecelia, our plane is over there," Uncle Jack said, pointing to a rickety old plane that looked as if it had been built by the Wright brothers. "Vintage" was the word Uncle Jack used. "Decrepit" was the word I thought of. As I looked at the plane's peeling paint, I started to feel a little sick.

The pilot stepped up to greet us wearing a huge grin. If he saw my worried look, he didn't give any sign. He helped me into the tiny passenger seat, buckled me up, and took his place at the controls. What followed was the absolute worst hour of my life. Right after we took off, I felt my stomach moving into my throat. I broke into a sweat. Then he banked the plane and made a sharp turn. My face turned green. He kept yelling, "Isn't this great?" as he performed one nose dive after another. I closed my eyes to black out the farmland spinning outside the window. Then he did a loop-the-loop, and I completely lost it. They probably heard my scream over in Chicago.

Finally the ride was over. The plane landed with a couple of bumps and skidded to a stop. My uncle Jack's beaming face lost its smile when he saw me. As he helped me from the plane, my legs felt like rubber. On the ride home, I wanted to thank my uncle for the special present, but I couldn't. It wasn't just that I still felt sick. It was more that I didn't understand how an experience that seemed like it would be so good could turn out to be so awful.

Complete these items about the personal narrative on page 26.

1. Find a sentence that indicates the writer is using **first-person point of view**. Circle a personal pronoun in it that refers to the writer.

2. What does the writer tell readers at the **beginning** of this narrative?

   _____

3. What does she describe in the **middle** of the narrative?

   _____

4. How does she **end** the narrative?

   _____

5. Circle words that tell **when** events happened. Draw a box around one word that tells **where** an event happened.

6. Underline two words that help the reader understand **the order in which events happened**.

7. Draw two lines under a sentence in which the writer tells about her **feelings**.

Write a Personal Narrative

Now you'll have a chance to write a personal narrative of your own. In your narrative, tell about an experience you had in which you did something for the first time. You can use the narrative on page 26 as a model.

1. **Plan**

Under **topic ideas**, write down two to four first-time experiences you might like to write about.

   topic ideas

   _____   _____

   _____   _____

Now circle the idea you like best. Then make some notes under the word **sequence**. Write down the events you will tell about, in the order they happened.

   sequence

   first   _____   next   _____
   then   _____   after that _____

2. **Write**

Write your personal narrative on another piece of paper. Use your notes to guide you.

3. **Reread and Correct**

After you have finished your narrative, read through it carefully. Look for mistakes in spelling. Look up any words you are not sure of. Think about the paragraphs you wrote. Did you begin a new paragraph each time there was a change in scene, idea, or speaker? Make corrections to your writing. If you want, you can make a clean copy of your corrected narrative.

Name_____   Perfect Score 52   My Score _____

LESSON 22
Unit II Review

1. On the lines below, write sentences using the words   **Handbook Guides 14, 20, 33, 35, 39**
    in parentheses. (Score: 7)

    (nothing) _____

    (haven't) _____

    (don't) _____

    (never) _____

    (may) _____

    (learned) _____

    (aren't) _____

2. In the following sentences, underline the words that   **Handbook Guides 1b–e, 2a–c, 2f, 2h,**
    should be capitalized and add necessary punctuation   **9, 11, 12**
    marks. (Score: 39)

    who watched michael jordan on TV this saturday asked gail

    gina said that she had watched him in the playoffs

    gail do you think jordan is the best athlete in the united states asked laverne

    well he is the greatest player in the history of the national basketball association she said

    suddenly gina shouted i have a great idea

    she said that they should create their own pro basketball Web site

3. On the lines below, write sentences using the verbs in   **Handbook Guide 21**
    parentheses. (Score: 6)

    (took) _____

    (did) _____

    (seen) _____

    (came) _____

    (went) _____

    (written) _____

LESSON 23
Identifying Parts of a Friendly Letter

PART I   Name the parts of the following letter. Write the name of each part on the numbered lines leading to it. (Score: 5)

1. _____   851 48th St.
   Sacramento, CA 95819
   February 20, 1999

2. _____   Dear Rich,

   I'm sorry, but I won't be able to buy your guitar.

3. _____   I just can't afford to pay what you're asking for it.

   If you decide that you'd be willing to sell it for less,

   please let me know and I'll count my money again.

4. _____   Your friend,

5. _____   Lesley

PART II   On the lines below write a short letter that Rich might wish to send to reply to Lesley. Be sure to include all the parts of a friendly letter. (Score: 25–5 for each part properly placed and appropriately capitalized and punctuated)

_____

_____

_____

_____

_____

_____

_____

_____

_____

_____

_____

Name_____   Perfect Score 20   My Score _____

LESSON 24
Addressing Envelopes

Handbook Guides 7a–c, 32

Address the following envelopes, using abbreviations for social, academic, or professional titles and other words where appropriate. Place your return address in the upper left-hand corner of each envelope. Remember to use postal code abbreviations for the names of states when addressing envelopes.

PART I   Address this envelope to Mister Lars Johnson, 7109 North Kelleher Avenue, Apartment 103, Houston, Texas 77001. (Score: 10—5 for each part appropriately written)

```

```

PART II   Address this envelope to Miss Joan Goldman, 1442 South Winston Avenue, Boulder, Colorado 80301. (Score: 10–5 for each part appropriately written)

```

```

Name_____ Perfect Score 10 My Score _____

UNIT
III

LESSON 25
Writing a Friendly Letter

Handbook Guides 28, 30

A friendly letter may tell about several different topics. Put each new topic in a separate paragraph.

On the lines below, write two short paragraphs that you could send as part of a letter to a good friend who lives in another place. Write each paragraph about something you're both interested in. You might want to write one paragraph about a good movie you've seen and then talk about family news in the second paragraph. You might want to discuss sports, your plans for a job, or mutual friends—whatever you talk about when you see your friend. Be sure to discuss only one subject in each paragraph. (Score: 10—5 for each paragraph)

_____

Optional Exercise: On another piece of paper, write a letter to a friend that includes the paragraphs you have just written. Be sure to use proper form and correct capitalization and punctuation. If you wish, you may mail the letter to your friend. See Handbook Guide 32 for information on how to address an envelope properly.

Name_____   Perfect Score 56   My Score _____

LESSON 26
Capitalization and Punctuation

Rewrite the following sentences, adding necessary capital letters and punctuation marks (commas, end marks, and quotation marks). (Score: 56)

1. i read an interesting article in a fashion magazine _____

    _____

2. it was about a chinese american fashion designer named anna sui _____

    _____

3. anna sui grew up in detroit michigan _____

    _____

4. she always wanted to be a fashion designer _____

    _____

5. ms sui attended parsons school of design in new york _____

    _____

6. for years she struggled to make a living sewing her designs in her apartment _____

    _____

7. isn't ms sui known for mixing different styles _____

    _____

8. her big break came when she won the perry ellis award _____

    _____

9. don't you think this outfit would look great on me i asked my friend_____

    _____

10. i wish i could be a fashion designer she exclaimed _____

    _____

11. anna sui has worked hard to become a success at the occupation she loves i replied ____

    _____

LESSON 27
Recognizing Nouns

Handbook Guide 15

A noun names a person, a place, a thing, or an idea.

PART I   Underline the nouns in the following sentences. (Score: 50)

Example: *Cooperstown, New York,* is a famous old *village.*

1.   Cooperstown lies at the foot of Otsego Lake.

2.   In early times the Mohicans called the lake *Ote Saga.*

3.   Cooperstown is named after William Cooper.

4.   His son, James Fenimore Cooper, was a famous novelist.

5.   Many people have read his book *The Deerslayer.*

6.   Two characters in his books are Hawkeye and Uncas.

7.   Cooperstown has five museums.

8.   Fenimore House is a museum of art and history.

9.   Farmers' Museum has a collection of tools used by pioneers.

10. The best-known museum is the National Baseball Hall of Fame and Museum.

11. Baseball was played in Cooperstown early in the nineteenth century.

12. Many people believe that Abner Doubleday invented the game.

13. Doubleday may have created the shape of the playing field.

14. Players are elected to the Hall of Fame by sportswriters.

15. The National Baseball Museum has many interesting exhibits.

16. There are also photographs of the national champions for each year.

17. The oldest photograph shows the Cincinnati Red Stockings.

PART II   Write five sentences of your own about a sport that interests you. Underline the nouns that you use in the sentences. (Score: 15–3 for each sentence)

18. _____

19. _____

20. _____

21. _____

22. _____

Name _____   Perfect Score 37   My Score _____

LESSON 28
Writing Plural Forms of Nouns

Study the example given before each group below to discover how plural nouns in that group are formed. Then write the plural form of each word. (Score: 37)

girl _____*girls*_____   key _____*keys*_____

1. pioneer _____   19. journey _____

2. rocket _____   20. joy _____

3. orchard _____   21. donkey _____

4. product _____   22. valley _____

5. canal _____   23. monkey _____

6. prairie _____   hobby _____*hobbies*_____

7. river _____   24. factory _____

8. mountain _____   25. bakery _____

church _____*churches*_____   26. colony _____

9. beach _____   27. dairy _____

10. wish _____   28. city _____

11. class _____   29. country _____

12. speech _____   30. fly _____

13. bunch _____   31. berry _____

14. fox _____   32. penny _____

ox _____*oxen*_____   loaf _____*loaves*_____

15. woman _____   33. knife _____

16. man _____   34. half _____

goose _____*geese*_____   35. shelf _____

17. foot _____   36. wolf _____

18. tooth _____   37. leaf _____

LESSON 29
Writing Possessive Forms of Nouns

> **Handbook Guide 17**
>
> Form the possessive of a singular noun by adding an apostrophe and an *s (dog's tail)*. When a plural form ends in *s*, add only an apostrophe *(boys' club)*. When a plural form does not end in *s*, add an apostrophe and an *s (men's hats)*.

PART I   On each line, write the possessive form of the word at the left. After it, write a noun that names something owned or possessed. (Score: 10)

Examples: miner   _____*miner's lamp*_____

buses   _____*buses' windows*_____

oxen   _____*oxen's hides*_____

1.   cat _____   6.   pilot _____

2.   engines _____   7.   mechanic _____

3.   flower _____   8.   men _____

4.   passengers _____   9.   doctors _____

5.   children _____   10.   managers _____

PART II   Rewrite each of the following phrases in possessive form. (Score: 4)

Example: wings of an eagle   _____*an eagle's wings*_____

11.   the speed of the wind   _____

12.   the achievements of the people   _____

13.   the book belonging to a friend   _____

14.   the picture of the twins   _____

PART III   Write the possessive form of each name in parentheses. (Score: 4)

Example: (Ms. Thompson) _____*Ms. Thompson's*_____ truck

15.   (Mrs. Weaver) _____ home

16.   (Gil) _____ raincoat

17.   (Dr. James) _____ office

18.   (Marlins) the _____ new pitcher

Name_____   Perfect Score 18   My Score _____

LESSON 30
Identifying Sentence Subjects

Handbook Guides 45a, b

The noun that tells what a sentence is about is the simple subject of the sentence. The simple subject may be compound—that is, made up of two or more nouns.

PART I   Underline the simple subject in each of the following sentences. (Score: 13)

Examples: Every spring the <u>buzzards</u> return to Hinckley, Ohio.

<u>Americans</u> and <u>Canadians</u> come to Hinckley for this big event.

1.   These birds always return to a spot called Buzzard's Roost.

2.   This spot is in the Hinckley Nature Reservation.

3.   Every year a festival marks the return of the birds.

4.   The day is called Buzzard Sunday.

5.   It begins with breakfast at a school.

6.   Townspeople and visitors gobble pancakes and sausages.

7.   Food and gifts are sold by local groups.

8.   Buzzards made of chocolate are also sold.

9.   These candies have red icing on their beaks.

10.   Parents and children enjoy buzzard cookies.

11.   T-shirts and buttons with buzzards are quite popular, too.

12.   Cars, trucks, and buses have buzzard bumper stickers.

13.   Sometimes people are treated to a film about buzzards.

PART II   Write nouns for the simple subjects of the sentences below. (Score: 5)

14.   In springtime _____ and _____ bloom and grow again.

15.   The _____ and _____ melt in the warm sunshine.

16.   In Hinckley _____ and _____ get out their binoculars.

17.   These _____ are watching for buzzards.

18.   Many _____ enjoy the return of the big birds.

Connecting Meanings   _____

Draw a line from each word in row 1 to its meaning in row 2. Then write a sentence using each word in row 1.

Row 1	reserve	preserve	deserve
Row 2	set aside	be worthy of	protect

LESSON 31
Punctuating and Writing Sentences

Handbook Guides 1c–e, 7d, 9, 11, 12, 13a, 17

PART I   Rewrite the following sentences, adding punctuation marks. (Score: 21)

1.   Nina brought out drop cloths brushes scrapers and metal ladders _____

_____

_____

2.   Allie do you know how to paint around window glass asked Nina _____

_____

_____

3.   No Nina I don't replied Allie _____

_____

4.   Then she said I will scrape away the cracked paint _____

_____

5.   Marcos remarked that Allies idea was a good one _____

_____

PART II   Following the instructions below, write short sentences of your own and punctuate them. (Score: 15–3 for each sentence)

6.   Write a sentence with three words in a series. _____

_____

7.   Write a sentence that contains a name in direct address and a possessive noun. _____

_____

8.   Write a sentence that includes a city and state written together. _____

_____

9.   Write a direct quotation. _____

_____

10.   Write an indirect quotation. _____

_____

UNIT III

LESSON 32
Writing a Problem/Solution Paragraph

Read a Problem/Solution Paragraph

> **Handbook Guide 28**
>
> **A problem/solution paragraph states a problem and explains how it was solved. Its purpose is to inform readers.**

Whether you know it or not, you're solving problems all the time. Some are small and easy to solve. Others are more difficult and require clever solutions. To explain to others the process of solving a particular problem, you can write a **problem/solution** paragraph. Here are some tips for writing this kind of paragraph:

- Describe the **problem** in the first part of the paragraph.

- Make sure to include enough **details** and **background information** to help readers understand why it was important for you to solve the problem.

- In the second part of the paragraph, describe the **solution**. Tell exactly what you did to solve the problem. If solving the problem took several steps, tell about these steps in order.

- Solutions aren't always perfect. If you like, you can end your paragraph by telling how you felt about the solution you came up with.

Read this example of a problem/solution paragraph:

How I Got to the World Series

I was born in New York City, and I lived there until I was 10. I rooted for all the home teams—the Knicks, the Giants, the Jets, the Mets, and the Yankees. When my family moved to Atlanta, I immediately adopted the Hawks, the Falcons, and the Braves, but I still cheered for my old teams. You can imagine how excited I was when the Braves and the Yankees both won their divisions and league championships in 1996. It meant they would play each other in the World Series. I would have done anything to get tickets to that series. I faced two stumbling blocks, though. First, the tickets were sold out. Second, even if I could find a ticket for sale, I didn't have the money to pay for it. My situation seemed hopeless. Then I came up with a plan. I had enough money to put an ad in the *Atlanta Journal* for a week. My sister helped me write it. It said, "Desperate Fan Needs World Series Ticket—Will Do Yard Work for One Year in Exchange." I never really expected to get a call, but I did. An older guy named Mr. Henry had two season tickets. His wife was in the hospital and couldn't go with him to the World Series games. The offer of free yard work convinced him to give me a call. That's how I got to see Game 3 of the 1996 World Series. (The Yankees won, 5-2!) Of course, I raked, trimmed, hoed, and mowed quite a lot that year, but it was worth every bit of work to see my favorite teams play each other in the World Series.

Complete these items about the problem/solution paragraph above.

1. What problem did the narrator face?

_____

2. Underline the sentences that state the problem.

3. Put stars by the sentences that describe the solution.

4. The narrator gave some background information that helps the reader understand why getting the ticket was so important. Circle the sentences that give this information.

5. Does the narrator seem to think that his solution was a good one, even though it resulted in a lot of work? Why or why not? _____

Write a Problem/Solution Paragraph

1. **Plan**

First, think about some problems you have solved. Here are some ideas to get you started:
- a transportation problem
- a problem with a friend
- a misunderstanding with someone
- a problem about money for a special event

Write two of your own problem-solving experiences on the lines. Then circle the one you want to write about.

_____

_____

Now plan your paragraph. Make notes on the lines below.

Background Information _____

_____

Problem _____

_____

Solution _____

_____

How You Felt
About the Solution _____

2. **Write**

Write your paragraph on another sheet of paper. Remember that when you're writing about a personal experience, you should use the first-person voice. Use your notes to guide you.

3. **Reread and Correct**

Reread your writing. Did you describe the problem in the first part of the paragraph? Did you describe the solution in the second part of the paragraph? Have you spelled each word correctly? Make any corrections needed. If you like, you can make a clean copy of your corrected paragraph.

Name_____ Perfect Score 28   My Score _____

LESSON 33
Unit III Review

1.   On the lines below, write four sentences. Underline | Handbook Guides 15, 45a
     each noun you have used. Then draw a second line
     under the noun or nouns that are the subjects of the sentences. (Score: 4)

_____

_____

_____

_____

2.   On the lines below, write a direct quotation and an | Handbook Guides 1b, 2h, 9
     indirect quotation. (Score: 2)

_____

_____

3.   In the first column below, write the plural form of the | Handbook Guides 16, 17
     word in parentheses. In the second column write the
     singular possessive form of the word. In the third column write the plural possessive
     form of the word. (Score: 18)

(stream)   _____   _____   _____

(sash)   _____   _____   _____

(woman)   _____   _____   _____

(turkey)   _____   _____   _____

(body)   _____   _____   _____

(life)   _____   _____   _____

4.   In the box below, address an envelope to a friend or | Handbook Guides 7a–c, 32
     relative. (Score: 4)

```
┌─────────────────────────────────────────────┐
│                                               │
│                                               │
│                                               │
│                                               │
│                                               │
│                                               │
│                                               │
│                                               │
└─────────────────────────────────────────────┘
```

Perfect Score 44   My Score _____

LESSON 34
Identifying Nouns and Pronouns

Handbook Guides 15, 18a

A noun names a person, a place, a thing, or an idea. A pronoun is a word that takes the place of a noun.

PART I   Underline the nouns in the following sentences. (Score: 28)

Example: Tiger Woods beat many famous golfers.

1.   Many people play golf on the weekends.
2.   People must have patience to play golf well.
3.   Good golfers must also train hard.
4.   Top players usually learn the game at an early age.
5.   Tiger Woods is such a person.
6.   As a young boy, Tiger watched his father play.
7.   Tiger grew up in Cypress, a town in southern California.
8.   This young man has won some very big tournaments.
9.   Nancy Lopez is a fine player, too.
10.   For many years Nancy was ranked among the best players.
11.   Many young golfers admire Ms. Lopez.

PART II   In the following sentences, pronouns have been substituted for some of the nouns in the sentences in Part I. Underline the pronouns in the sentences below. (Score: 16)

Example: He beat them.

12.   They play golf on the weekends.
13.   They must have patience to play it well.
14.   They must also train hard.
15.   They usually learn it at an early age.
16.   He is such a person.
17.   As a young boy, he watched him play.
18.   He grew up in Cypress, a town in southern California.
19.   He has won them.
20.   She is a fine player, too.
21.   For many years she was ranked among the top players.
22.   They admire her.

Optional Exercise: List the pronouns in the sentences in Part II. Then beside each pronoun write the noun that it replaced.

Name_____   Perfect Score 25   My Score _____

LESSON 35
Using Pronouns as Subjects

> **Handbook Guides 18b, 18e**
>
> The subject pronouns are *he, I, she, they,* and *we.* The pronouns *it* and *you* may also be used as subjects. Subject pronouns are used after the verbs *is* and *was.* Pronouns may be used in pairs, or a pronoun may be paired with a noun.

PART I   Underline the appropriate pronouns in parentheses. (Score: 8)

1. Dub and (me, I) have been hired to work in the auto plant.

2. (She, Her) and (I, me) are welders.

3. (We, Us) will work the third shift.

4. (She, Her) learned to weld from her brother.

5. (Them, They) used to work together in a body shop.

6. (He, Him) and (me, I) were once in a metal shop class together.

PART II   Underline the appropriate pronoun to use after *is, am,* or *was.* (Score: 5)

7. Dub asked, "Is (she, her) the new supervisor?"

8. "Yes, I am (she, her)," said the woman in gray.

9. Was it (she, her) who saved someone last week?

10. No, it was (them, they) who pulled the injured worker free.

11. It certainly was not (I, me).

PART III   Fill the blanks with subject pronouns. There is more than one way to complete each sentence. (Score: 12)

12. _____ and _____ are the ones who weld the floors to the frames.

13. _____ is welding trunk lids today.

14. You and _____ have much to learn about auto assembly.

15. It is _____ who really wants a job.

16. Was it _____ who was promoted?

17. Yes, and _____ will probably be promoted again soon.

18. _____ and _____ caused the assembly line to be shut down.

19. Dub and _____ were very angry.

20. _____ and _____ take pride in our work.

Optional Exercise: Write sentences using the subject pronouns in Part I.

LESSON 36
Using Pronouns after Verbs and Prepositions

Handbook Guides 18b–d

The pronouns *her, him, me, them,* and *us* are used after action verbs. They are also used after prepositions, such as *beside, by, for, from, to,* and *with.*

PART I   Underline the appropriate pronoun in parentheses. (Score: 14)

1. Our magazine sent Verna and (I, me) to cover the Turkey Trot in Cuero, Texas.
2. The people of Cuero were very friendly to (she, her) and (I, me).
3. A journalism class asked for a visit from (her, she) and (me, I).
4. Eating turkey chili was a treat for Verna and (me, I).
5. A young friend taught (we, us) a dance called the Turkey Trot.
6. Verna wanted me to stand with (her, she) and another photographer.
7. But a different spot gave (she, her) and (I, me) a better look at the festivities.
8. Two people invited (she, her) and (I, me) to the big race.
9. Our new friends told (we, us) that a turkey from Cuero would race a turkey from Worthington, Minnesota.
10. We helped (they, them) cheer Cuero's speedy turkey on to victory!

PART II   On each line below, write a short sentence, using the pronoun in parentheses after an action verb. Use a different verb in each sentence. (Score: 4)

Example: (us) _____ *The people told us more about the good old days.* _____

11. (them) _____
12. (her) _____
13. (us) _____
14. (me) _____

PART III   On each line below, write a short sentence, using a pronoun after the preposition in parentheses. Use a different pronoun in each sentence. (Score: 4)

Example: (beside) _____ *One of the players sat beside us.* _____

15. (to) _____
16. (for) _____
17. (from) _____
18. (with) _____

Odd Word Out _____

Circle the word in this list that does not belong with the others. Name a category that would fit the four uncircled words. Then name a category for the word you circled.

rhyme   haiku   statue   verse   sonnet

Name_____   Perfect Score 21   My Score _____

LESSON 37
Using Pronouns

Handbook Guides 18a–f

The pronouns *he, I, she, they,* and *we* are used as subjects. The pronouns *her, him, me, them,* and *us* are used after action verbs and also after prepositions. **When you use *we* or *us* with an explaining noun after it (*we boys, us girls*), remember that *we* is the subject form and that *us* is used after action verbs and prepositions.**

PART I   Fill each blank with the appropriate form, *we* or *us.* (Score: 6)

1.   Mr. Kamada told _____ about Halley's Comet.

2.   _____ won't be able to see it until 2061.

3.   Can a tour of Lick Observatory be arranged for _____ visitors?

4.   Yes, _____ astronomers can do that.

5.   Next spring _____ will buy a new telescope.

6.   All of _____ can point out the major constellations.

PART II   Substitute pronouns for the underlined words. (Score: 15)

Example: The upstairs neighbors are using our star chart.

_____*They*_____ are using ___*it*___.

7.   Alexander and Linda Sue know about Halley's Comet.

_____ and _____ know about _____.

8.   Dolores told Alex and Linda Sue to come to the roof.

_____ told _____ and _____ to come to the roof.

9.   Was it Dolores and Alex who saw a shooting star?

Was it _____ and _____ who saw a shooting star?

10.   Linda Sue and Alex read that new book about stars.

_____ and _____ read that new book about stars.

11.   Alex asked Dolores to point to Taurus and Aries.

_____ asked _____ to point to _____.

12.   Now Dolores is looking for Gemini and Cancer.

Now _____ is looking for _____ .

Name_____   Perfect Score 20   My Score _____

LESSON 38
Using I and Me

Handbook Guides 18a–e, 18g, 18h

The pronoun *I* is a subject pronoun. The pronoun *me* is used after an action verb or a preposition.

When *I* or *me* is used with other pronouns or nouns, *I* or *me* is placed last.

PART I Write the correct pronoun, *I* or *me*, in each blank. (Score: 11)

1. Fred and _____ visited the salmon cannery.

2. It was _____ who wanted to see a cannery.

3. A guide showed some complicated machines to Fred and _____.

4. _____ asked most of the questions.

5. The guide told Fred and _____ about the canning process.

6. Sue and _____ watched the workers canning salmon.

7. She told _____ to look at the bright orange and blue labels on the cans.

8. One of the workers gave her and _____ some labels as souvenirs.

9. That worker also wrapped up some cans of salmon for Fred and _____ to take home.

10. Yes, it is _____ whom you see in that picture of the cannery.

11. The guide asked Fred, Sue, and _____ to sign the visitors book.

PART II Underline the appropriate word group in parentheses. (Score: 9)

12. (Sue and I, I and Sue) knew that salmon spawn in fresh water.

13. (She and I, I and she) learned that the fish deposit eggs on riverbeds.

14. A worker told (Fred and me, me and Fred) that the fish later swim to the ocean.

15. The guide took (me and Sue, Sue and me) to see the Columbia River salmon.

16. (She and I, I and she) saw workers bringing in the salmon.

17. The guide showed (me and her, her and me) how the fish are caught.

18. (Me and her, She and I) saw a salmon jump up a six-foot-high waterfall.

19. The workers showed (her and me, she and I) a picture of a huge salmon.

20. (Sue and I, I and Sue) enjoyed learning about the life cycle of salmon.

UNIT IV

LESSON 39
Eliminating Unnecessary Sentences in Paragraphs

> **Handbook Guide 28a**
>
> A paragraph should tell about a single topic.

In each of the following paragraphs there are three sentences that do not tell about the topic introduced in the first sentence. Draw a line through each of those sentences. (Score: 30—5 for each sentence properly marked out)

The Hazards of City Driving

People who drive in a city must watch out for many things. They must watch out for other cars, for people on foot, and for bicycle riders. I'd never buy a car without a radio. If a driver sees a ball bounce into the street, he or she should slow down. It's possible that a child will race out after the ball. It's not easy to pass your first driver's test. Holes in the street are another type of hazard drivers must be careful to avoid. Driving over a pothole can ruin a car's suspension system. A new paint job can make an old car pleasant to drive again.

They Were the Worst

The 1899 Cleveland Spiders were the worst major league baseball team in history. Baseball is often called the national pastime. The Spiders won only 20 games and lost 134. Why were they so bad? It happened that their owner also owned the St. Louis major league team during 1899. St. Louis is the largest city in Missouri. The owner traded Cleveland's good players to St. Louis for St. Louis's bad players. As a result, St. Louis did well and Cleveland did very poorly. Other team owners were angry at what happened, so they decided to make a rule that no one would be allowed to own more than one major league team. The 1996 New York Jets football team had a poor record, too.

Word Whiz _____

Use the clues on the left to help you complete the words on the right. Use a dictionary for spelling help.

change to something else	__ __ __ v e r t
turn upside down	__ __ v e r t
change the course of	__ __ __ v e r t
return to the way it was	__ __ v e r t

LESSON 40
Replacing Nouns with Pronouns

Handbook Guides 18, 28

The paragraph below needs to have some proper nouns changed to pronouns so it does not sound so repetitive. Read the paragraph silently. Then rewrite it on the lines below, changing some of the nouns to pronouns. Use subject pronouns as sentence subjects. Use object pronouns after verbs and prepositions. (Score: 12—1 for each pronoun used correctly)

      Jill decided to have a party at the skating rink. Jill invited Ray, Annette, and Robyn to the party. Ray and Annette accepted immediately. Ray and Annette really love to skate. Robyn did not respond to the invitation right away. Finally, though, Robyn called Jill to accept the invitation. Jill assured Robyn that Robyn would have fun. Afterward, Robyn was glad Robyn decided to go to the party. Robyn had a great time! Jill taught Robyn how to skate backwards, and Ray and Annette performed some amazing jumps. Ray landed a double toe loop, and Annette landed a double axel! Robyn later told Ray and Annette that Ray and Annette were the best skaters Robyn had ever seen.

_____

_____

_____

_____

_____

_____

_____

_____

_____

_____

_____

_____

_____

Name_____   Perfect Score 41   My Score _____

LESSON 41
Eliminating Unnecessary Words

Handbook Guide 40

PART I   Draw a line through each unnecessary word. There may be more than one unnecessary word in each sentence. (Score: 32)

Aladdin

1. Aladdin he like wandered through the streets all day long.

2. One day a magician went and said to him, "Aladdin, I am your uncle."

3. Then the magician asked, "Where is your father at?"

4. "My father he is dead," Aladdin answered.

5. The magician said he would go and visit the boy's home.

6. After a while the magician went and took the boy to the country.

7. "Where are we going to?" asked Aladdin.

8. "Come on with me, and you will see," the magician replied.

9. Later the magician said, "Pick up these here sticks and make a fire with them."

10. The magician he like threw some magic powder on the fire.

11. The earth it like opened suddenly, and a cave thing appeared.

12. The magician told Aladdin to go and get a lamp off of a shelf in the cave.

13. He went and gave the boy a magic ring to keep him like safe.

14. Aladdin took the lamp off of the shelf, but he would not give it up to the magician.

15. The magician he angrily closed that there cave with Aladdin inside it.

16. Aladdin went and rubbed the ring the magician had given him.

17. A great genie like rose up and took him out of that there cave.

PART II   Rewrite the sentences below, omitting the unnecessary words. (Score: 9)

18. Aladdin he like went and hurried home and showed his mother the lamp. _____

_____

19. When she like tried to clean it by rubbing it, another genie appeared. _____

_____

20. That there genie helped Aladdin go and become like very rich. _____

_____

LESSON 42
Capitalization and Punctuation

Handbook Guides 1b–d, 2a, 2b, 2f, 2h, 4, 8, 9, 12, 13a, 14, 17a, 17b

PART I   Underline each word that should begin with a capital letter. Add necessary punctuation marks. (Score: 55)

1.   yesterday i finished reading one of bonnies books about colorado history

2.   its called *the life of an ordinary woman*

3.   it was written by anne ellis

4.   the book is about life in the old-time colorado mining towns

5.   anne ellis lived for a long time in the san luis valley

6.   this valley is bounded by the sangre de cristo mountains on the east

7.   farms in this high fertile rocky valley fed the gold miners

8.   a steep road led up from the valley to bonanza sedgwick exchequerville and kerber city

9.   villa grove was the main town in the san luis valley

10. its store had a sign offering fresh eggs rubber boots and corsets

PART II   Rewrite the following sentences properly. (Score: 50)

11. bonnie asked did you enjoy ms elliss sense of humor _____

_____

12. i replied yes i really did _____

_____

13   in the book, ms ellis said i'd gone up the gulch at six and come down at sixteen _____

_____

14. ms ellis called one road a rare specimen of engineering skill bonnie said _____

_____

15. she said that a vehicle could get over it without upsetting bonnie continued _____

_____

16. what a gritty person ms ellis must have been i said _____

_____

UNIT IV

Name_____

LESSON 43
Writing a Persuasive Paragraph
Read a Persuasive Paragraph

Handbook Guide 18a

The purpose of a persuasive paragraph is to convince others to agree with you.

When you write to try to convince people to agree with you about something, you create a **persuasive paragraph**. Here are some tips for writing a persuasive paragraph:

- State your **opinion** in the first sentence of the paragraph.
- In the body of the paragraph, give **facts** that support your opinion. Remember that a fact is a statement that can be proven.
- Include some reasons that will appeal to readers' **emotions**. You may want to use **emotional words** such as *unjust*, *outrageous*, and *terrible* in stating these reasons.
- In the last part of the paragraph, restate your opinion. Then give a **call to action**. Tell your readers what they can do!

Read this example of a persuasive paragraph:

A Good Decision

The Fairfield Unified School District board members have approved a regulation requiring all students in elementary and middle schools to wear uniforms starting next year. I feel that this change will be good, for many reasons. First, it will stop competition in dressing. Some students come from families that have the money to buy them the latest styles, but others don't. The school board took a poll this year. They found that many of the kids who don't have expensive athletic shoes, logo jackets, and other fashion items feel bad about not having the same cool clothes other kids have. I think it's terribly sad that some kids feel embarrassed because they don't have hundred-dollar shoes and designer jeans. Also, uniforms will save time and effort. Shopping for clothes for school takes many hours of students' and parents' time. Buying uniforms requires only one or two shopping trips a year. Uniforms also are easier to wash and last longer than a lot of trendy clothes. School should be for learning, not for comparing fashions. For the reasons above, I think school uniforms in Fairfield is a wise idea. It will make school life a lot easier for parents, teachers, and students. If you agree, write to the school board and tell them you support their decision.

Complete these items about the persuasive paragraph above.

1. Underline two sentences that state the writer's **opinion** about school uniforms.

2. Where in the paragraph do these sentences appear? _____

3. Put stars by the **facts** the writer has used to support her opinion.

4. Underline the sentences that appeal to readers' **emotions**. Circle two **emotional words** the writer has used.

5. What does the writer tell readers to do in the last sentence?

_____

Write a Persuasive Paragraph

Now you'll have a chance to write your own persuasive paragraph. Use the paragraph on page 50 as a model. Follow these steps to plan and write your paragraph.

I. Prewriting

A   Choose a Topic. Choose a topic that is important to you. It's easier to write persuasively if you have strong feelings about the topic. You might write about a rule or law you think is unfair. You could write about an issue in your school or community. Or, you could write in support of a person who is at the center of a controversy. Write down two to four topic ideas on another sheet of paper. Circle the one you like best.

B   Plan Your Paragraph. Make notes on the lines below to help you plan what you'll say in each part of the paragraph. As you plan, think about the people whom you are trying to convince. Choose reasons that will appeal to that audience.

First Part of the Paragraph: State Opinion

_____

Body of the Paragraph: Present Facts

Fact #1: _____

Fact #2: _____

Fact #3: _____

Body of the Paragraph: Make an Emotional Appeal

_____

End of the Paragraph: Restate Opinion/Give a Call to Action

_____

II.   **Write a First Draft.** Use your outline to write a first draft of your persuasive paragraph. Do this on another piece of paper. Don't worry about mistakes. You'll have a chance to fix them later.

III.   **Revise.** Read over your first draft. Ask yourself these questions:

- Have I stated my opinion in the first part of the paragraph, and stated it again in the last part of the paragraph?
- Does the body of the paragraph contain facts? Do all the facts support my opinion?
- Have I used reasons and emotional words that will appeal to my audience?
- Have I given readers a call to action at the end?

Now make changes that will strengthen your argument.

IV.   **Proofread.** Do a final check of your work. Make sure you have spelled every word correctly. Make sure all of your sentences are complete.

V.   **Publish.** After you've corrected your paragraph, make a clean copy. Share your argument by sending it to the editor of your school or community newspaper. Or, read it aloud to classmates. Find out what they think about the topic.

Name_____ Perfect Score 28 My Score _____

LESSON 44
Unit IV Review

1. Write sentences using the words given in parentheses. `Handbook Guides 18a–h`
    (Score: 8)

    (she and I) _____

    (him and me) _____

    (her and him) _____

    (you and us) _____

    (you and he) _____

    (we) _____

    (she) _____

    (he and she) _____

2. Rewrite each sentence, substituting pronouns for the `Handbook Guides 18a–d`
    underlined words. (Score: 8)

    <u>Harry</u> and <u>Sue</u> enjoyed <u>the movie</u> very much. _____

    _____

    I saw <u>Sue and Harry</u> at the ice cream shop after <u>the show</u>. _____

    _____

    <u>Mr. Friedkin</u> talked to <u>Sue</u> about <u>her new job</u>. _____

    _____

3. Draw a line through the unnecessary words in the `Handbook Guide 40`
    following sentences. (Score: 12)

    Steven Spielberg he is a great director.

    Where was *Amistad* filmed at?

    Is this here theater showing *Jurassic Park?*

    I've seen that movie like at least five times.

    Jurassic Park it has got amazing special effects.

    I like love it when the eggs open to reveal baby dinosaurs.

    Remember when the Tyrannosaurus rex he like tears the roof off of a shed?

    We'll go and ride the Jurassic Park ride at Universal Studios this summer.

LESSON 45
Writing Titles with Names

PART I   Rewrite the names below, using the proper social, academic, or professional title before each name. If the title can be abbreviated, use the abbreviation. (Score: 10)

Example:
James J. Ricelli (an electrician)   _____*Mr. James J. Ricelli*_____

1. Gladys T. Faatui (a high school senior)   _____

2. Mary Anne Abdallah (a married woman)   _____

3. Helen Magid (a dentist)   _____

4. T. Y. Wong (a state governor)   _____

5. Karla Christensen (a judge)   _____

6. Andrew O'Connell (a doctor)   _____

7. Lee S. Sieminski (a professor)   _____

8. Connie Branca (a sergeant in the army)   _____

9. Rodney M. Jones (a senator)   _____

10. Sue L. Enomoto (a scientist)   _____

PART II   Write the names of the following persons, using the appropriate title before each name. Abbreviate those titles that can be abbreviated. (Score: 6)

11. the president of the United States   _____

12. the governor of your state   _____

13. a senator from your state   _____

14. the mayor of a city in your area   _____

15. a member of the clergy in your community   _____

16. one of your teachers   _____

Odd Word Out _____

Circle the word in this list that does not belong with the others. Name a category that would fit the four uncircled words. Then name a category for the word you circled.

representative   banker   mayor   governor   President

UNIT V

LESSON 46
Writing a Business Letter—Inside Address and Greeting

Rewrite each of the following inside addresses in appropriate form. Below each address write a proper greeting. (Score: 13—1 for each line)

Handbook Guide 31

A business letter has the five parts of a friendly letter and also an inside address. An inside address is the name and address of the person who will receive the letter. The greeting of a business letter is followed by a colon.

Examples:

Dr. Raymond Weiss
Macias Medical Group
728 Wells Building
Akron, OH 44309

Dear Dr. Weiss:

Perreault Printer Co.
1552 Larch Street
Ames, IA 50010

Dear Service Manager:

1. Miss Joan Donaldson, 1442 Third Street, Gilroy, CA 95020

_____

_____

_____

_____

2. Primo Auto Painting, 1880 Lincoln Avenue, Cleveland, OH 44101

_____

_____

_____

_____

3. Mr. A. B. Guliford, Rest-a-Sured Motel, 1723 Ebenezer Street, Cedar Rapids, IA 52401

_____

_____

_____

_____

Name_____   Perfect Score 56   My Score _____

LESSON 47
Writing a Business Letter—Form

Handbook Guides 2a, 2f, 31

On the lines below, rewrite the following business letter, arranging the parts properly. Add necessary capital letters and punctuation. (Score: 1 for each punctuation mark or capital letter properly used and 4 for each part of the letter properly placed)

21 althoff avenue lansing michigan 48900 june 8 1999 electric automobile magazine 5500 market street tyler texas 75701 dear editor i sent for the free copy of your magazine. your ad said that i did not have to pay unless i wanted to order the magazine. now you have sent me a bill for a year's subscription. i will not pay this bill because i did not order a subscription sincerely yours pat sims

_____

_____

_____

_____

_____

_____

_____

_____

_____

_____

_____

_____

Word Whiz _____

Use the clues on the left to help you complete the words on the right. Use a dictionary for spelling help.

Clue	Word
tell all about	__ __ s c r i b e
write an order for a medicine	__ __ __ s c r i b e
sign up to receive a magazine regularly	__ __ __ s c r i b e

UNIT
V

LESSON 48
Writing a Business Letter

Answer one of the advertisements below. Include all parts of the business letter and arrange them properly. Use your own address in the heading. (Score: 5 for each part of the letter properly placed and written with correct capitalization and punctuation)

For a free catalog of our radio-controlled model boats, write Magic Miniboats, Box A-775, Trenton, New Jersey 08609.

Send $2.00 for plans for making your own canvas day pack. Sizes S-M-L-XL. The Ridge Ranger Company, 645 Gale Boulevard, Roanoke, Virginia 24001

_____

_____

_____

_____

_____

_____

_____

_____

_____

_____

_____

_____

_____

_____

_____

_____

_____

LESSON 49
Dividing Words into Syllables

Handbook Guides 44a, 44b

In a two-syllable word the sound of the first vowel determines where the word is divided. If the first vowel has a long sound, the word is divided after the vowel (*la-dy, du-plex*). If the first vowel has a short sound, the word is divided after the consonant following the first vowel (*mel-on, thun-der*).

PART I   Divide each word below into two syllables according to the example given above each column. In each word of the left column, the first vowel is long. In each word of the right column, the first vowel is short. (Score: 20)

Example:

soda	*so-da*	winter	*win-ter*
1. paper	_____	11. wagon	_____
2. table	_____	12. camel	_____
3. vacant	_____	13. medal	_____
4. cedar	_____	14. pencil	_____
5. locate	_____	15. solid	_____
6. secret	_____	16. figure	_____
7. pirate	_____	17. punish	_____
8. pony	_____	18. minute	_____
9. donate	_____	19. sentence	_____
10. bugle	_____	20. comic	_____

PART II   Divide the following words into syllables, paying particular attention to the sound of the first vowel in the word. (Score: 12)

21. rifle	_____	27. robin	_____
22. river	_____	28. lemon	_____
23. labor	_____	29. bonus	_____
24. music	_____	30. fever	_____
25. bundle	_____	31. cabin	_____
26. silent	_____	32. under	_____

Name_____   Perfect Score 38   My Score _____

LESSON 50
Using Homophones

Handbook Guide 25
Homophones are words that sound the same but have different meanings.

PART I   Underline the word that fits the meaning of the sentence. (Score: 32)

1. (Whose, Who's) the person who wrote the song "Hello, Walls"?

2. Willie Nelson is a singer (whose, who's) songs stick in a listener's mind.

3. Would you like to (hear, here) one of his records now?

4. (Here, Hear) is the album that has "(Blue, Blew) Eyes Crying in the Rain" on it.

5. Willie Nelson is a singer (whose, who's) music has been called "outlaw country" and "redneck rock."

6. But (its, it's) really a blend of country, blues, folk, Western swing, and honky tonk music.

7. Where Willie Nelson lives, the (son, sun) shines hot in the summer.

8. You probably (no, know) that Austin and San Antonio are in central Texas.

9. The wind (blue, blew) very hard when we passed (through, threw) there.

10. Hasn't Willie Nelson (won, one) Grammy Awards for his singing and songwriting?

11. He's a (grate, great) guitar player, (too, two, to).

12. He was taught (too, two, to) play guitar (by, buy) his grandparents.

13. He is also the (son, sun) of a guitar player.

14. (Your, You're) welcome to borrow these (too, two, to) albums.

15. You can (see, sea) his gray (hare, hair) and beard in the pictures on the album.

16. I think I'll (by, buy) some (new, knew) strings for my guitar.

17. I'm learning (too, two, to) play (won, one) of Willie Nelson's songs.

18. Isn't "Crazy" (won, one) of (your, you're) favorite tunes, (too, two, to)?

19. (No, Know), I don't (no, know) how to play the steel guitar.

20. (It's, Its) strings are tuned differently than those of a six-string guitar.

21. Someday I'll (meet, meat) someone who can teach me to play it.

PART II   Write sentences using the words in parentheses. (Score: 6)

22. (stares)   _____

23. (stairs)   _____

24. (cent)   _____

25. (sent)   _____

26. (weak)   _____

27. (week)   _____

LESSON 51
Using Lie *and* Lay

> **Handbook Guide 34**
>
> **The verb *lie* means "to rest, recline, or remain in one place." The verb *lay* means "to put or place something."**

PART I In each blank, write the appropriate form of the verb *lie* (*lie, lies, lying, lay, lain*). In deciding which form to use, look for words in the sentence that indicate the time when the action takes place. (Score: 11)

A Sore Subject

1. Yesterday I saw a moon jellyfish _____ on the beach.

2. I had been _____ peacefully on my towel.

3. Suddenly I noticed an odd, gooey blob _____ near me.

4. Fran said, "That is a moon jellyfish _____ there beside you."

5. "How long do you think it has _____ there?" I asked.

6. "It has _____ there long enough to lose its sting," she continued.

7. "I'm glad it isn't dangerous, but I will _____ down somewhere else," I said.

8. I asked Fran whether jellyfish ever _____ still in the water.

9. "I don't think a jellyfish ever _____ motionless," Fran said.

10. Rick was _____ on an air mattress out in the surf.

11. His right arm _____ where a blueplate jellyfish could sting it.

PART II In each blank, write the appropriate form of the verb *lay* (*lay, lays, laying, laid*). (Score: 7)

12. "Where did you _____ my snorkel yesterday?" asked Nick.

13. "I _____ it on a piece of driftwood," said Ida.

14. "You shouldn't have _____ it there," Nick replied.

15. "Why did you _____ it where it could be washed away?" Nick continued.

16. Ida said, "Ceil and Jay are _____ out their beach mats on the sand now."

17. Nick asked, "Why didn't we _____ out our mats near the pier?"

18. Ida said, "Mats shouldn't be _____ where sand fleas are leaping."

Name_____   Perfect Score 22   My Score _____

LESSON 52
Choosing Standard Verb Forms—
Lie *and* Lay

PART I In the sentences below, underline the appropriate form in parentheses. In deciding which form to use, think about which verb—*lie* or *lay*—gives the appropriate meaning in the sentence. (Score: 14)

1. I saw an old sign (lying, laying) behind Bonnie's bookcase.

2. I picked up the sign and (laid, lay) it on the table.

3. Dust (lay, laid) thick upon the once-colorful picture on the sign.

4. The picture showed a person (lying, laying) inside a long wooden box.

5. A woman dressed in black had just (laid, lain) down a saw.

6. The woman had (lain, laid) it down because she had finished sawing the box in half.

7. I asked Bonnie why the sign had been (lying, laying) in her office.

8. "A great career once (lay, laid) ahead of me," she said sadly.

9. She took a cape out of a box and (laid, lay) it on the table.

10. Then I realized why the sign had (lain, laid) there.

11. Bonnie must have (laid, lain) it there after she stopped performing as a magician.

12. "Would you (lay, lie) down inside that steamer trunk for a minute?" she asked.

13. "I know exactly where I (lain, laid) my saw," she continued.

14. I didn't (lay, lie) down, though, because I wasn't ready to be sawed in half.

PART II Write sentences using the words in parentheses. (Score: 8)

15. (laid)   _____

16. (lying)   _____

17. (lies)   _____

18. (lain)   _____

19. (lays)   _____

20. (laying)   _____

21. (lie)   _____

22. (lay)   _____

LESSON 53
Capitalization and Punctuation

Handbook Guides 1b–e, 2a, 2b, 2d, 2f–h, 3, 7d, 8a, 9, 10a, 10c, 11, 12

PART I Underline each uncapitalized word that should begin with a capital letter. Add necessary punctuation marks. (Score: 91)

The American Revolution

1. val can you tell us when the First Continental Congress met asked the instructor

2. i think it met on september 5 1774 said val

3. elena said patrick henry was at that meeting in philadelphia pennsylvania

4. what happened to crispus attucks in boston massachusetts asked the instructor

5. he was an african american who was shot by british soldiers said louis

6. elena said paul revere warned americans that the british were coming

7. the instructor said h w longfellow wrote a famous poem about paul revere's ride

8. on june 17 1775 a famous battle was fought in massachusetts said val

9. oh that was the battle of bunker hill exclaimed elena

10. louis said abigail adams made many important reports about british troops and ships

PART II Rewrite the following sentences, using appropriate capitalization and punctuation. (Score: 20—5 for each sentence written properly)

11. louis do you know who led the american attack on fort ticonderoga asked val _____

_____

12. yes it was ethan allen replied luis _____

_____

13. louis added that he had read a book called <u>america's ethan allen</u> _____

_____

14. elena explained that mercy warren was another who helped to win independence for

america _____

_____

Name_____

LESSON 54
Writing a Paragraph of Information
Read a Paragraph of Information

Handbook Guide 28

A paragraph of information gives facts about a single topic. Its purpose is to inform readers about the topic.

Whenever you need to inform people about an event, a place, a project, or some other topic, you can write a **paragraph of information**. Here are some tips for writing this kind of paragraph:

- Begin your paragraph with a **topic sentence** that tells what the whole paragraph is about.

- In the body of the paragraph, give **supporting details** that tell more about the topic.

- Include **facts**, not opinions, in your paragraph.

- Include **details** that will be useful for your readers to know. If you need to, look up additional information in an encyclopedia or in another book.

- Explain any **unfamiliar terms** you use.

Read this example of a paragraph of information:

Urban Bandits

Raccoons are a familiar sight in city neighborhoods nowadays. If raccoons have moved into your neighborhood, there are a few things you should know. The raccoon is a nocturnal animal, which means it's active mostly at night. It prowls city streets, alleys, and backyards between dusk and dawn in search of food. In the wild, raccoons eat berries, insects, and small animals such as frogs. In the city, they eat anything they can find. This includes pet food, the contents of garbage cans, and earthworms, which they dig up in gardens. Raccoons have clever paws. They can open garbage cans, smash jars on pavement, and open pet doors. City raccoons usually are not shy, and if one is cornered it will fight its way out. Raccoons can snarl and bark somewhat like dogs, and they have sharp teeth and claws. If you have a raccoon family in your neighborhood, you can enjoy observing them at night—from a distance! Also, make sure the lid to your garbage can is closed tightly and your pet door is locked!

Complete these items about the paragraph of information above.

1. What is the topic of the paragraph? _____

2. Draw a line under the topic sentence.

3. Where in the paragraph does that sentence appear? _____

4. Put an X by each fact the writer has included.

5. The writer used the word *nocturnal* in the third sentence. Find the words that explain what this term means. Write them here.

_____

6. The writer has given facts about raccoons' physical features. He has also given facts about what raccoons can do. Write some of these details on the lines below.

Physical Features   Abilities

1._____   1. _____

2._____   2. _____

Write a Paragraph of Information

Now write your own paragraph of information. Write about an animal you have spent some time observing. You could write about a wild animal or a pet. Use the paragraph on page 62 as a model.

1. Plan

First, pick a wild animal or pet you want to describe. Choose an animal you know well or have observed on many occasions. Write its name at the top of the organizer below.

Then think of some facts and details about the animal. Try to answer these questions: What are the animal's physical features like? What can the animal do? Write your ideas in the organizer.

Animal:	
Physical Features:	**Abilities:**

2. Write

Write your paragraph of information on another piece of paper. Use your notes to guide you.

3. Reread and Correct

Reread your writing. Does your paragraph have a topic sentence? Have you included facts and details about the topic? Have you explained unfamiliar words? Make necessary corrections. Then, if you like, make a clean copy of your corrected paragraph of information.

UNIT V

LESSON 55
Unit V Review

1. On the lines below, write four social, academic, or professional titles. If the title can be abbreviated, write the abbreviation after the title. (Score: 8)

Handbook Guide 4

_____   _____

_____   _____

2. Write sentences using the words in parentheses. (Score: 6)

Handbook Guide 34

(lie) _____

(lay) _____

(laid) _____

(lain) _____

(lying) _____

(laying) _____

3. On the lines below, write a greeting and a complimentary close that would be proper in a business letter. (Score: 2)

Handbook Guide 31b

_____   _____

4. Divide the following words into syllables. (Score: 4)

Handbook Guides 44a, 44b

title _____   member _____

grumble _____   robot _____

5. On the lines below, write sentences using the words in parentheses. (Score: 6)

Handbook Guide 25

(its) _____

(it's) _____

(there) _____

(their) _____

(weak) _____

(week) _____

LESSON 56
Choosing Standard Verb Forms

Handbook Guides 20, 21, 33–35

PART I   Underline the correct verb in parentheses. (Score: 18)

"Snowshoe" Thompson

1. Telemark, Norway, (was, were) the birthplace of Joe Tostenson Rue.

2. Joe (learned, taught) how to ski when he was very young.

3. He and his parents (come, came) to America in 1837.

4. In 1849, 1850, and 1851 many people (gone, went) west to California.

5. Joe Tostenson Rue (come, came) to California to pan for gold.

6. Months of failure (learned, taught) him that gold was hard to find.

7. During this time he (began, begun) to use a new name.

8. He had (began, begun) to call himself John Thompson.

9. He also (become, became) an American citizen.

10. Then Thompson settled in the Sacramento Valley and (began, begun) ranching.

11. However, John Thompson (wasn't, weren't) happy with this life.

12. Some mountaineers (is, are) never happy on the flatlands.

13. Then a newspaper (ran, run) an ad for a mail carrier.

14. Wagons (wasn't, weren't) able to cross the mountains in winter.

15. Few mail carriers (has, have) ever had such a difficult route.

16. During the next twelve winters, snow almost always (lay, laid) thick on the mountains.

17. "Snowshoe" Thompson (flew, flown) over the snow fields on his long skis.

18. (Can, May) you imagine how cold it was in those mountains?

PART II   Write sentences using the words in parentheses. (Score: 7)

19. (known)   _____

20. (done)   _____

21. (ate)   _____

22. (written)   _____

23. (learned)   _____

24. (laid)   _____

25. (knew)   _____

Name_____ Perfect Score 28   My Score _____

LESSON 57
Using Pronouns

Handbook Guides 18a–h, 45h

PART I   Underline the correct form in parentheses. (Score: 19)

1. Today the four of (we, us) are recording sound effects.
2. Alison and (me, I) are now making animal noises.
3. All of (we, us) must use imagination.
4. (We, Us) sound engineers rattle a tin sheet to make the sound of thunder.
5. Stacy is lending her tape recorder to Alison, Mac, and (me, I).
6. It was also (her, she) who lent (we, us) the editing software.
7. (She, Her) expects (we, us) to be careful with her equipment.
8. A real challenge has been presented to (we, us).
9. A TV station has asked (me and Alison, Alison and me) to make a soundtrack.
10. (Them, They) want sounds for a program about auto safety.
11. Stacy will help (she, her) and me with this project.
12. What can (Alison and I, I and Alison) do to make car crash sounds?
13. It was (I, me) who suggested dropping pie pans, old glass, and sandbags.
14. (We, Us) must be very careful doing this.
15. Between you and (I, me), I would rather run the tape machine.
16. Then Stacy will come, and Alison will help Mac and (she, her) mix the sounds.
17. (Alison and I, I and Alison) won't have any trouble recording a car screech.

PART II   Following the instructions below, write short sentences of your own. (Score: 9—3 for each sentence)

18. Write a sentence containing a pronoun after *is*.

   _____

19. Write a sentence containing a pronoun after *of* or *with*.

   _____

20. Write a sentence using the pronoun *we* as the subject.

   _____

Find the Goof _____

Correctly rewrite the sentence in which the boldfaced word is used improperly.

The sound of the **herd** is deafening.

I have not **herd** a word you have said.

LESSON 58
Using Apostrophes in Possessives and Contractions

Handbook Guides 14, 17

An apostrophe is used in making the possessive form of a noun. It is also used to show where one or more letters are omitted in a contraction.

PART I   Write the possessive form of each noun below, and after it write something that the noun may possess. (Score: 8)

1. nation _____
2. Ms. Azarin _____
3. Charles _____
4. children _____
5. friends _____
6. Lucy _____
7. guitar _____
8. Minnesota Vikings _____

PART II   Write the contractions of the words below. (Score: 8)

9. I had _____
10. you will _____
11. they have _____
12. I am _____
13. it is _____
14. I will _____
15. we are _____
16. I have _____

PART III   The following sentences may be written two ways, depending on the contraction you use. Rewrite each sentence both ways. (Score: 6)

Example:

   She is not using her skateboard today.

   She isn't using her skateboard today.
   She's not using her skateboard today.

17.   They are not afraid of falling.

   _____

   _____

18.   It is not easy to jump over a broomstick.

   _____

   _____

19.   I hope you are not planning to go down that hill.

   _____

   _____

LESSON 59
Using Your *and* You're; There, Their, *and* They're

Handbook Guide 25

Your and *their* are possessive pronouns. *You're* and *they're* are contractions for *you are* and *they are*. *There* can be used as a noun, adverb, adjective, or interjection.

PART I Write the appropriate form, *your* or *you're*, in each blank. (Score: 4)

1. _____ going to have interesting dreams tonight.

2. _____ community center is showing *The Creature from the Black Lagoon*.

3. Yes, _____ coming with us.

4. This movie will make _____ flesh crawl.

PART II Write the appropriate form, *there*, *their*, or *they're*, in each blank. (Score: 11)

5. _____ are two other movies playing in town this weekend.

6. The theater owners are doing _____ best to scare everyone.

7. _____ showing *Frankenstein* and the original *King Kong*.

8. Millions have had _____ blood chilled by Boris Karloff as the Frankenstein monster.

9. The poster _____ on my wall shows Fay Wray in King Kong's hand.

10. _____ is nothing like watching three good horror films in one weekend.

11. Has _____ ever been an uglier monster than the creature from the black lagoon?

12. The people in the audience won't believe _____ eyes.

13. _____ likely to scream until they lose _____ voices.

14. I can hardly wait until we get _____ .

PART III Write sentences using the words in parentheses. (Score: 5)

15. (your) _____

16. (you're) _____

17. (there) _____

18. (their) _____

19. (they're) _____

LESSON 60
Using Possessive Pronouns

PART I   Write the possessive form of the pronoun in parentheses. Remember to capitalize words that begin sentences. (Score: 12)

1.   (I) _____ family comes from Boone County, Iowa.

2.   (he) My father spent _____ childhood there.

3.   (you) Do you remember any stories _____ parents used to tell?

4.   (we) One of _____ favorites was about young Kate Shelley.

5.   (she) Kate risked _____ life to save the lives of many passengers on a train.

6.   (they) On July 6, 1881, the Shelleys were huddled in _____ farmhouse.

7.   (I) According to _____ father, the Shelleys were waiting out a heavy storm.

8.   (they) _____ house was near the two bridges across Honey Creek.

9.   (it) The railroad bridge was sagging because _____ pilings had weakened.

10.   (they) A crew was out in _____ engine looking for washouts.

11.   (she) The family heard a crash, and Kate looked at _____ mother.

12.   (they) _____ senses told them the railroad bridge had collapsed under the train's weight.

PART II   Underline the appropriate form in parentheses. (Score: 8)

13.   Soon the midnight express was to make (it's, its) run along the same tracks.

14.   "(There's, Theirs) a chance I can warn the express," Kate said to herself.

15.   "But (it's, its) miles to the station, and (there's, theirs) a bridge to cross," she thought.

16.   (It's, Its) very dangerous to cross a wet bridge in a storm.

17.   After crossing, she thought, "(There's, Theirs) still a quarter mile to go."

18.   (It's, Its) a good thing that Kate reached the station in time to halt the train.

19.   The passengers learned that a tragic fate was not to be (there's, theirs).

Optional Exercise: Write sentences using the possessive pronouns *my, your, his, her, our, their,* and *its.*

Name_____ Perfect Score 16 My Score _____

LESSON 61
Using *Them, These,* and *Those;*
Himself, Herself, and *Themselves*

> **Handbook Guides 18a, 18c, 18d, 18i, 41**
>
> The words *these* and *those* are used to point out persons or things. Do not use the pronoun *them* before a noun to point out persons or things.
>
> The word *these* points out persons or things that are nearby. The word *those* points out persons or things that are farther away.
>
> Always use *himself, herself,* or *themselves*—never *hisself* or *theirselves.*

PART I Fill in the blank with the proper word in parentheses. (Score: 11)

1. (them, those) Why are you carrying all _____ signs?

2. (these, them) I have to give _____ signs to our neighbors.

3. (these, them) Are _____ campaign buttons yours, too?

4. (them, those) Yes, _____ buttons are mine.

5. (These, Them) _____ pamphlets tell about the candidate I'm working for.

6. (these, them) You should read over _____ news accounts.

7. (them, those) Do you really agree with all _____ accounts?

8. (these, them) Yes, _____ plans will certainly help our city.

9. (these, them) I'm enjoying working with _____ people on this campaign.

10. (Them, Those) _____ other candidates have many supporters, too.

11. (them, those) Well, we are leading _____ other candidates in the latest poll.

PART II Write the appropriate form, *himself, herself,* or *themselves,* in each blank. (Score: 5)

12. This speech was written by Mrs. Dusek _____.

13. She left the reporters to talk among _____.

14. With this speech, she won votes for _____.

15. One opponent, Mr. Bly, made a fool of _____.

16. Some of the other candidates may be angry with _____.

Antonym Watch _____

Circle the word in the second row that is an antonym of a word in the first row. Then draw a line connecting the two words.

Row 1	deny	detect	detest
Row 2	afford	affirm	amend

LESSON 62
Choosing Standard Verb Forms—
Sit *and* Set

Handbook Guide 36

Sit means "to be seated." *Set* means "to place or put."

PART I Fill each blank with the proper word, *sit, sits, sitting, sat, set, sets,* or *setting.* (Score: 15)

1.   Last week I _____ in the library and read about smoke alarms.

2.   Finally I _____ the book on the desk.

3.   Iris, _____ here for a moment.

4.   Watch while I _____ this smoke alarm against the wall.

5.   Should I _____ it against the ceiling instead?

6.   Did I _____ the drill on the table?

7.   From where you _____, how does it look?

8.   You are _____ on the instructions, Alberta.

9.   Don't _____ the ladder too close to the stairs.

10. Soon I'll be _____ the smoke alarm in place.

11. Shouldn't you _____ it near the bedroom door?

12. Let's _____ up smoke alarms in every room.

13. Now we won't _____ up all night worrying about fire.

14. A smart family _____ rope ladders inside second-floor rooms.

15. A fire extinguisher now _____ near our kitchen stove.

PART II Write sentences using the words in parentheses. (Score: 6)

16. (sat)   _____

17. (sitting)   _____

18. (sets)   _____

19. (sits)   _____

20. (setting)   _____

21. (sit)   _____

LESSON 63
Giving Details in Sentences

Handbook Guide 28b

Include details in sentences to give the reader a clearer picture and to make what you are saying more interesting.

By adding details, rewrite the sentences below so that they will give a clearer picture of what is being described. Read all six sentences before you start writing. Try to imagine what you would see and hear if you were one of the people involved. (Score: 5 for each sentence)

Example:

The guard walked into the warehouse.

The short, tough-looking guard walked silently into the dark warehouse.

1. He saw a light flash behind some boxes.

   _____

   _____

2. The guard's heart began to thump.

   _____

   _____

3. His partner was asleep in the car.

   _____

   _____

4. The partner heard a call for help.

   _____

   _____

5. She walked into the warehouse.

   _____

   _____

6. She heard footsteps, and she turned around.

   _____

   _____

LESSON 64
Capitalization and Punctuation

PART I   Underline each word that should begin with a capital letter. Add necessary punctuation marks. (Score: 87)

1. cassie said i need a book to read on friday lucinda

2. have you read a book called *black elk speaks* yet asked lucinda

3. cassie said no i dont think i have

4. it was written by john g neihardt said lucinda

5. it was based on his visit with black elk she continued

6. was black elk a member of one of the dakota tribes asked cassie

7. lucinda replied yes he was one of the oglala sioux

8. the dakota once rode the plains from canada to the black hills cassie remarked

9. black elk was a wise person and a spiritual leader said lucinda

10. he was second cousin to crazy horse she continued

PART II   Rewrite the sentences below, using proper capitalization and punctuation. (Score: 39)

11. where did mr neihardt meet with black elk asked cassie

    _____

    _____

12. lucinda said they met on the pine ridge reservation in south dakota

    _____

    _____

13. im going to read about black elk said cassie

    _____

    _____

14. then she asked did you know that my fathers grandmother was a member of a dakota tribe

    _____

    _____

Name_____

LESSON 65
Writing a Paragraph About a Process
Read a Paragraph About a Process

Handbook Guide 28

A paragraph about a process explains how something is made or done. Its purpose is to inform readers.

When you explain how something is made or done, you are creating a **process explanation**. Knowing how to describe a process can help you share your own knowledge with others. It can also help you complete assignments at school and on the job. Here are some guidelines for writing a paragraph about a process:

- Name the process you're describing in the first sentence.

- Give the steps in order. Use **sequence words** such as *first*, *next*, and *then* to help make the order clear.

- If you need to use special terms, explain what they mean for the reader.

- Conclude the paragraph by describing the finished product.

Read this example of a paragraph about a process:

How Pottery Is Made

Making handmade pottery is a process that requires six separate steps. First, a potter slices off a hunk of clay small enough to work with. Clay contains air bubbles, which can cause a pot to crack or break when it is heated. Before shaping the clay, the potter must get the air bubbles out by pressing, kneading, and pounding the clay. This is called wedging. Next, the potter places the mound of clay in the very center of the potter's wheel. Then the potter sits at the wheel to shape the clay. As the wheel spins, the potter shapes the clay by pressing and pulling the spinning mass. Once the clay has been formed into the desired shape, the potter removes it from the wheel and sets it aside to dry for several days. After that, the potter puts the dried pot in a special oven called a kiln. As the kiln heats up, the clay pot hardens. This is called a bisque firing. The pot is still not finished, though. It must then be dipped in special paint called glaze and fired in the kiln a second time. The finished pot is sturdy, shiny, and beautiful.

Complete these items about the explanation above.

1. Underline the sentence that names the process the writer is describing.

2. Reread the paragraph and think about the order of the steps. Write the numbers 1–6 next to the steps below to show the order in which each step is done.

   ____wedge the clay   ____shape the clay on the potter's wheel

   ____fire the pot the second time   ____fire the pot the first time

   ____glaze the pot   ____let the pot dry

3. Circle three sequence words or phrases the writer has used in the paragraph to help make the order clear.

4. Underline three special terms the writer has used to describe the process. Then write one of these terms below. Also give its meaning.

term: _____

meaning: _____

Write a Paragraph About a Process

Now you'll have a chance to describe a process. In your explanation, tell how something is made. You can draw on your own personal knowledge. Or, you can get information from a how-to video, a book, or a magazine.

1. **Plan**

Pick a process that can be explained in a paragraph. "How a Battleship Is Built" is too big a topic. You might describe how fingernails are painted, how chocolate chip cookies are made, or any other process that interests you. Write your topic on the line below.

Topic: How _____

Next, write the steps in the process. Add additional steps on another piece of paper, if you need to. You may need to look in a reference source to find information.

1. _____
2. _____
3. _____
4. _____
5. _____
6. _____

Circle any special terms. You'll need to explain what they mean when you write your paragraph.

2. **Write**

Write your paragraph on another sheet of paper. Use your notes to help you.

3. **Reread and Correct**

Reread your writing. Ask yourself these questions:

- Did I name the process in the first part of the paragraph?
- Did I explain the steps in order?
- Did I use sequence words to make the order clear?
- Did I give the meanings of special terms?
- Have I spelled each word correctly?
- Did I describe the finished product?

Make any necessary corrections. Copy your corrected paragraph on a clean sheet of paper.

LESSON 66
Unit VI Review

On the lines below, rewrite the following paragraphs, using appropriate verbs, pronouns, and homophones. (Score: 22)   Handbook Guides 14, 17, 18, 20, 21, 25, 34, 36

When your riding a bicycle, you must always watch the rode ahead of you. When us friends driven to work yesterday, we seen an accident in front of Mrs Wilsons store. A cyclist weren't paying attention to the cars parked along the street. A driver opened a car door, and the cyclist run write into it. He crumpled to the pavement, and his head striked the cement. Fortunately, he was wearing a safety helmet.

The driver of the car thrown a jacket across the cyclist and set beside him until the traffic officer come. When the ambulance arrived, the medics lied the cyclist on a stretcher and taken him to the hospital. Someone said that the cyclists leg was broke. The officer taken the names of we people who had saw the accident.

_____

_____

_____

_____

_____

_____

_____

_____

_____

_____

_____

_____

_____

LESSON 67
Using a Dictionary—
Alphabetical Order

PART I Arrange the following words in alphabetical order. (Score: 9)

gulf   dock   ocean   city   television   forest   zoology   radar   history

1. _____   4. _____   7. _____

2. _____   5. _____   8. _____

3. _____   6. _____   9. _____

PART II Arrange the words below in alphabetical order. Arrange the words that begin with the same letter according to the second letter. (Score: 9)

ancient   artist   altitude   bay   boundary   burden   curtain   clothes   camera

10. _____   13. _____   16. _____

11. _____   14. _____   17. _____

12. _____   15. _____   18. _____

PART III Arrange the words below in alphabetical order. Arrange the words that begin with the same two letters according to the third letter. (Score: 9)

better   bench   beside   certain   center   cello   donate   doughnut   dollar

19. _____   22. _____   25. _____

20. _____   23. _____   26. _____

21. _____   24. _____   27. _____

PART IV Arrange the words below in alphabetical order. Arrange the words that begin with the same three letters according to the fourth letter. (Score: 9)

chart   champion   chance   drill   drift   drive   employ   emperor   empty

28. _____   31. _____   34. _____

29. _____   32. _____   35. _____

30. _____   33. _____   36. _____

UNIT VII

LESSON 68
Using a Dictionary—Spelling and Pronunciation

Handbook Guides 42, 43, 44

PART I Underline the correctly spelled word in each pair. Use a dictionary; do not guess. (Score: 10)

1.	similar	similiar	6.	lenght	length
2.	finaly	finally	7.	privilege	priviledge
3.	peacable	peaceable	8.	receive	recieve
4.	makeing	making	9.	coming	comming
5.	height	hight	10.	beleive	believe

PART II Divide each of the following words into syllables. Place an accent mark after the syllable that should be stressed. Use a dictionary to find out where each word should be divided. (Score: 18)

Example:

discover   _dis-cov´er_

11.	atlas	_____	20.	holiday	_____
12.	express	_____	21.	develop	_____
13.	zebra	_____	22.	remember	_____
14.	remove	_____	23.	wonderful	_____
15.	terror	_____	24.	happiness	_____
16.	delight	_____	25.	elegant	_____
17.	thunder	_____	26.	community	_____
18.	arrange	_____	27.	biology	_____
19.	apartment	_____	28.	impossible	_____

PART III In most dictionaries the pronunciation of a word is given after the entry word. Write the pronunciation of each word below as given in your dictionary. (Score: 8)

29.	reign	_____	33.	growth	_____
30.	rough	_____	34.	chemist	_____
31.	grimy	_____	35.	physics	_____
32.	cheek	_____	36.	cello	_____

LESSON 69
Using a Dictionary—Finding Information

Use a dictionary to find the answers to the following questions. Write your answers on the lines provided.

1. Is a *newt* a reptile or an amphibian? _____

2. How many sides does a *pentagon* have? _____

3. The word *rodeo* comes from what language? _____

4. A *Hoosier* is a person born in what state? _____

5. How many legs does a *quadruped* have? _____

6. Which word sounds like *lein*—*lean* or *lane*? _____

7. Does a *payee* make payment or receive payment? _____

8. How many inches equal a *meter*? _____

9. How many syllables does the word *candlestick* have? _____

10. Where is the accent mark placed in *drowsy*? _____

11. Which word describes age—*miner* or *minor*? _____

12. What does *Pan* mean in *Pan-American*? _____

13. The English sport of *rugby* is like what American sport? _____

14. Which word means part of a meal—*desert* or *dessert*? _____

15. Which syllable is stressed in the word *intermediate*? _____

16. The word *algebra* comes from what language? _____

17. How many syllables does the word *satisfactory* have? _____

18. What is a *soursop*? _____

19. How many feet are in a *mile*? _____

20. How is *bay* in *bayou* pronounced? _____

21. What does *in-* mean in *invisible* and *incomplete*? _____

22. A *merino* is a breed of what animal? _____

Name_____ Perfect Score 20 My Score _____

LESSON 70
Identifying Synonyms

Handbook Guide 26
Synonyms are words that have the same
or almost the same meaning.

PART I From the following list choose a word that is a synonym of each of the numbered
words below. Write the word on the line. (Score: 10)

inside	amusing	aid	demand
soft	weep	melody	raise
unusual	search	like	impolite
obtain	hilarious	labor	disgrace

Example:

funny _____*hilarious*_____

1. hunt   _____
2. within _____
3. get   _____
4. toil   _____
5. strange _____

6. help   _____
7. tune   _____
8. lift   _____
9. rude   _____
10. cry   _____

PART II Rewrite each of the following sentences, substituting a synonym for each of the
underlined words. (Score: 10)

Example:

The <u>lawn</u> was <u>strewn</u> with old cans.

_____*The grass was littered with old cans.*_____

11. Will we be able to <u>preserve</u> the <u>ancient</u> building?

_____

12. The <u>citizens</u> of our town <u>admire</u> that building.

_____

13. We have raised enough <u>cash</u> to <u>repair</u> it.

_____

14. A <u>capable</u> contractor is <u>leading</u> the project.

_____

15. I hope this <u>stately</u> building will stand <u>always</u>.

_____

LESSON 71
Identifying Antonyms

> **Handbook Guides 26, 27**
> **Antonyms are words with opposite meanings.**

PART I   Write an antonym for each of the following words. (Score: 18)

Example

up   *down*_____

1.	always	_____	10.	late	_____
2.	frown	_____	11.	happiness	_____
3.	back	_____	12.	accept	_____
4.	rise	_____	13.	many	_____
5.	arrive	_____	14.	idle	_____
6.	ending	_____	15.	dark	_____
7.	cowardly	_____	16.	before	_____
8.	strong	_____	17.	loose	_____
9.	nervous	_____	18.	full	_____

PART II   For each of the underlined words write a synonym in the first column and an antonym in the second column. (Score: 8)

	Example:	**Synonym**	**Antonym**
	a <u>hard</u> task	*difficult*	*easy*
19.	an <u>orderly</u> room	_____	_____
20.	an <u>ancient</u> car	_____	_____
21.	<u>above</u> the trees	_____	_____
22.	<u>purchase</u> a suit	_____	_____

Name That Job _____

Decide what occupation the person who uses these things probably has. Then write a paragraph telling how each item is used.

tractor   fertilizer   combine   silo

UNIT VII

LESSON 72
Choosing Correct Homophones

Handbook Guide 25

PART I   Underline the word that fits the meaning of the sentence. (Score: 38)

1. Have you (red, read) about the (great, grate) civilizations of long ago?

2. Many people (no, know) something about ancient Egypt and ancient (Greece, Grease).

3. (Sum, Some) people, however, do (knot, not) know about the ancient Maya.

4. (Their, There) are remains of Mayan cities in eastern Mexico, Guatemala, and Belize.

5. Today we (no, know) many things about (their, there) civilization.

6. (It's, Its) believed that they developed an accurate calendar about ten centuries ago.

7. The changing positions of the (sun, son), moon, and stars were studied (by, buy) the Maya.

8. The (some, sum) of the number of steps on (one, won) Mayan temple is 365.

9. Do you (no, know) what the number of steps represents?

10. If (your, you're) answer is the (daze, days) in (one, won) year, (your, you're) (right, write).

11. Uxmal and Chichén Itzá were (two, too, to) important Mayan cities.

12. Perhaps you have (herd, heard) (tails, tales) of the fierce games played (their, there).

13. (Their, There) are many who believe the ancient Maya were peaceful people, though.

14. (Would, Wood) you like (two, too, to) explore the Mayan temples?

15. You may (sea, see) a mysterious (red, read) hand mark inside (some, sum) of them.

16. You should visit the city of Mérida, (two, too, to).

17. (No, Know), a (weak, week) is not (two, too, to) much time to spend (their, there).

18. When was the last time you (eight, ate) fresh, delicious prawns?

19. Many visitors (by, buy) hammocks in Mérida.

20. You should walk (by, buy) the marketplace early in the morning.

PART II   Write sentences using the words in parentheses. (Score: 5)

21. (piece)   _____

22. (peace)   _____

23. (rode)   _____

24. (road)   _____

25. (rowed)   _____

LESSON 73
Identifying Adjectives and Adverbs

Handbook Guides 22, 23

An adjective describes a noun or a pronoun. An adverb describes a verb, an adjective, or another adverb.

PART I   Underline the adjectives in the following sentences. Do not underline the articles *a, an,* and *the.* (Score: 19)

Example:

> Can a person be a <u>great</u> artist and also a <u>skillful</u> leader?

1. Leopold Senghor was a wise, talented, and powerful person.

2. Senghor was the first president of the small African country of Senegal.

3. He was also a famous poet.

4. Senghor was born in the coastal town of Joal.

5. The early years of Senghor's life were pleasant and carefree.

6. This bright young person lived among skillful agricultural people.

7. He learned about the many unusual plants and wild animals of west Africa.

PART II   Underline the adverbs in the following sentences. (Score: 11)

Example:

> The first year of school was <u>very</u> difficult for Senghor.

8. He quickly had to learn a new language, French.

9. But Senghor gradually began to enjoy school.

10. He became extremely good at languages and mathematics.

11. Later he traveled to Paris.

12. He was consistently an outstanding student.

13. In Paris Senghor often shared ideas with students from Africa and the West Indies.

14. He began to express his ideas beautifully and forcefully in poetry.

15. Since that time Senghor has continually written great poetry.

16. Today many people remember him for ruling Senegal wisely.

PART III   Write sentences using the adjective and adverb in parentheses. (Score: 2)

17. (quietly)   _____

18. (funny)   _____

Name_____   Perfect Score 31   My Score _____

LESSON 74
Choosing Standard Forms

PART I   Underline the appropriate word in parentheses. (Score: 27)

1. In 1970 Lake Erie (was, were) a mess.
2. People in Michigan, Ohio, Pennsylvania, New York, and Canada (seen, saw) the problem.
3. A polluted lake (is, are) not easy to clean up, however.
4. Engineers (comes, came) to study Lake Erie, and they (took, taken) water samples.
5. The engineers (seen, saw) many signs of trouble.
6. Raw sewage was being poured (in, into) the lake.
7. Rivers full of industrial wastes (runs, ran) into Lake Erie.
8. The engineers also (taught, learned) that algae were partly to blame.
9. (Them, Those) little water plants (was, were) using up the oxygen in the lake.
10. Most fish (wasn't, weren't) able to live (in, into) the oxygen-poor lake.
11. Much work (went, gone) (in, into) the cleanup of Lake Erie.
12. No one can keep a lake clean by (himself, hisself) or herself.
13. (Doesn't, Don't) everyone need to understand the causes of pollution?
14. (We, Us) North Americans must work together to fight pollution on our continent.
15. What have people (did, done) to clean up Lake Erie?
16. New sewer pipes have been (lay, laid), and new treatment plants have been built.
17. Industrial waste standards have been (set, sat).
18. Some improvement (in, into) the quality of the lake waters has been (saw, seen).
19. But we shouldn't be holding (any, no) celebrations yet.
20. The waters of Lake Erie (is, are) still polluted.
21. The cost of making Lake Erie cleaner (is, are) high.
22. People must ask (theirselves, themselves) how much it is worth to have clean water.

PART II   Write sentences using the words in parentheses. (Score: 4)

23. (don't)   _____
24. (may)   _____
25. (into)   _____
26. (lain)   _____

LESSON 75
Capitalization and Punctuation

PART I   Underline each word that should begin with a capital letter. Add necessary punctuation. (Score: 84)

What's So Funny?

1. on tuesday february 18 1998 my friend hannah was snickering gurgling and howling

2. hannah whats so funny i asked

3. havent you looked through this book yet she asked

4. no ive never seen it before i answered

5. i noticed that the books title was *cat*

6. it was a book of cartoons by b kliban

7. i said hannah id like to borrow this book

8. oh im sorry she said

9. ive already promised it to ted rachel bill molly john heidi igor and connie she said

10. then she told me that she would show me her favorite drawing

11. it showed the difference between a cat and a meat loaf

PART II   Rewrite the following sentences, using proper capitalization and punctuation. (Score: 15—5 for each sentence properly written)

12. i told hannah that i didnt see the humor in the drawing _____

_____

13. but on february 20 1998 i looked at pureheart, our lazy Burmese cat _____

_____

14. i saw that pureheart did look a lot like a meat loaf _____

_____

Odd Word Out _____

Circle the word in this list that does not belong with the others. Name a category that would fit the four uncircled words. Then name a category for the word you circled.

solar   planet   asteroid   orbit   sonnet

Name_____

LESSON 76
Writing a Paragraph of Explanation

Read a Paragraph of Explanation

Handbook Guide 28

A paragraph of explanation is used to inform readers about a real-life topic or situation. This kind of paragraph can be useful at home, at school, and on the job.

You can write a paragraph of explanation whenever you need to inform someone about a real-life topic. Here are some tips:

- Begin the paragraph with a **topic sentence** that tells what you are explaining.

- Think about your **audience**, the people who will read the paragraph. Use words and ideas that will make sense to that audience.

- In the body of the paragraph, give a **complete explanation**. Try not to leave any important questions unanswered.

- Include both **facts** and **opinions**, if they are appropriate to your topic.

- Write a **concluding sentence** at the end of the paragraph that sums up your thinking.

Read this example of a paragraph of explanation:

Advice for Incoming Freshmen

The key to succeeding in high school is balancing schoolwork, social life, and other school activities. Giving all your time and energy to only one of these areas will deprive you of a full high school experience. Classes in high school can be very difficult. You'll have to pay attention in class and spend enough time on your homework if you're going to do well in your classes. Don't spend all your time studying, though. A big part of high school is making new friends and having fun. Many students find that a good way to meet people is by taking part in activities like sports, school clubs such as drama club, and community service. Don't be afraid to try new things; this may be your only chance to take metal shop or join a badminton team. High school is full of chances to learn and to make friends. Take advantage of the chance to experiment with different classes and unusual activities, because your four years in high school will be over before you know it.

Complete these items about the paragraph above.

1. What is the writer explaining in this paragraph?_____

   _____

2. Underline the sentence that tells what the paragraph is about.

3. What three things does the writer say must be balanced if a person is to succeed in high school?

   A. _____

   B. _____

   C. _____

4. Who is the audience for this paragraph? _____

5. What is one fact about high school the writer has included? _____

   _____

6. Put a star next to the sentence that sums up the explanation.

Write a Paragraph of Explanation

Now it's your turn to explain something in a paragraph. The steps below will help you.

1. **Plan**

   First, pick a topic. Here are some ideas. Add your own ideas on the lines. Then circle the topic you like best.

audience	**purpose**
parent(s) and relatives	explain how something broke
young children	explain the importance of wearing a bike helmet
friends your age	offer advice for improving a skill

   _____   _____

   _____   _____

   Write a topic sentence that tells what you are explaining.

   _____

   _____

   Write ideas for the body of the paragraph here. List them in an order that makes sense. You can include both facts and opinions. Use another sheet of paper if you need to.

   • _____

   • _____

   • _____

   • _____

   Finally, write a concluding sentence that sums up your explanation.

   _____

   _____

2. **Write**

Write your paragraph on another piece of paper. Use your notes to guide you. Remember to think about your audience, and use words and ideas that will make sense to that audience.

3. **Reread and Correct**

Reread your paragraph. Have you included a topic sentence and a concluding sentence? Is your explanation complete? Have you spelled every word correctly? Make any corrections needed. If you want, make a clean copy of the paragraph and give it to a person who is part of the audience for whom it was written.

Name_____   Perfect Score 40   My Score _____

LESSON 77
Unit VII Review

1. Pronounce each word below to yourself. Then divide   Handbook Guides 42, 44
    the word into syllables and place an accent mark after
    the syllable that should be stressed. (Score: 12)

    magnet   _____   propose   _____

    lightning _____   credit   _____

    major   _____   demand   _____

2. Alphabetize the words in each column below.   Handbook Guide 43a
    Alphabetize words that begin with the same letters
    according to the second, third, and fourth letters of the words. (Score: 18)

    chat   _____   stand   _____

    call   _____   sleep   _____

    chop   _____   stick   _____

    creek   _____   spare   _____

    cloud   _____   spring   _____

    crib   _____   slope   _____

    core   _____   spell   _____

    crest   _____   sting   _____

    coal   _____   slant   _____

3. Write *S* on the line beside each pair of synonyms   Handbook Guides 26, 27
    below. Write *A* on the line beside each pair of
    antonyms. (Score: 6)

    answer   reply   _____   carton   box   _____

    push   shove   _____   dull   sharp   _____

    over   under   _____   globe   sphere   _____

4. On the lines below write two sentences. Use two   Handbook Guides 22, 23
    adjectives in the first sentence. Underline these
    adjectives. Use two adverbs in the second sentence. Circle these adverbs. (Score: 4)

    _____

    _____

LESSON 78
Combining Sentences Using And

Handbook Guides 24a, 24b

On each line write one sentence, using *and* to combine the two short sentences. It may be necessary to change other words in the sentence, including the form of the verb.

Example:

Brenda sells real estate.
George sells real estate.   *Brenda and George sell real estate.*

1.   Realtors sell houses. Realtors sell condominiums. _____
_____

2.   Realtors must know neighborhoods. They must know property values. _____
_____

3.   Buyers are often anxious. Sellers are often anxious. _____
_____

4.   Realtors are always looking for listings. They are also always looking for buyers. _____
_____

5.   Sometimes realtors work two months and make nothing. Sometimes they work two
hours and make $10,000. _____
_____

6.   Buyers have different needs. Buyers have different tastes. _____
_____

7.   A realtor learns what people like. A realtor shows homes that fit their taste. _____
_____

8.   Ms. Mosley has a sunny personality. She also has years of experience selling real estate.
_____

9.   She showed us a four-bedroom home. She said it was a good buy. _____
_____

10.   That house was too large for us. It was too expensive. _____
_____

Name_____   Perfect Score 10   My Score _____

LESSON 79
Combining Sentences Using Connecting Words and Phrases

Combine each pair of short sentences below into one sentence by using one of the connecting words or phrases in the following list. (Score: 10)

but   when   if   until   although   as soon as   where   since   because
and   after   before   even though

Example: I like excitement. I decided to go rafting on the Colorado River.

Because I like excitement, I decided to go rafting on the Colorado River.

1. I arrived at the camp. A guide named Angela met me. _____
   _____

2. She showed me to my tent. I stowed my gear. _____
   _____

3. The cook made a great meal over the campfire. I didn't eat much. _____
   _____

4. I get nervous. I lose my appetite. _____
   _____

5. We finished dinner. Angela gave a talk on the history of the Grand Canyon. _____
   _____
   _____

6. John Wesley Powell began an exploration of the Colorado River canyons in 1869.
   He had four boats made. _____
   _____
   _____

7. Powell and his group traveled hundreds of miles on the river between steep canyon
   walls. They became the first non-native people to explore the Grand Canyon.
   _____
   _____
   _____

8. Powell's wooden boats were sturdy. They were not easy to maneuver. _____
   _____
   _____

9. Today most river runners use rubber rafts. They are easy to maneuver. _____
   _____
   _____

10. You don't know real fear. You've faced the 25-foot wave of Crystal Rapids. _____
    _____
    _____

LESSON 80
Rewriting Paragraphs

Rewrite the paragraphs below, combining the short sentences into longer, better ones. You may add adjectives and adverbs (or any other words you wish). You may also eliminate any words or phrases that don't add to the meaning. (Score: 30—10 for each paragraph rewritten appropriately)

This is about Imogen Cunningham. She was an American. She was a photographer. Many people think she was great. She began taking photographs in 1901. She continued to take them for more than seventy-five years.

Some of her pictures are realistic. Others aren't. These others show things that are strange and fantastic. She took pictures of people. She took pictures of interesting objects. She took pictures of plants. She is famous for her portraits of Hollywood movie stars. These were taken during the 1930s.

Imogen Cunningham's photographs have been displayed in many museums. These museums are all over the world. Her photos also appear in photography books. She truly was an artist. She was somebody who made art with a camera.

_____

_____

_____

_____

_____

_____

_____

_____

_____

_____

_____

_____

_____

_____

_____

Name_____   Perfect Score 26   My Score _____

LESSON 81
Using Contractions

PART I   Underline the proper word in parentheses. (Score: 24)

1.   (Doesn't, Don't) you get tired of reading about superstars?
2.   (Isn't, Aren't) you ready to read about somebody who (isn't, aren't) famous?
3.   Well, (hasn't, haven't) you heard of the one and only Raccoon Rae?
4.   It (doesn't, don't) surprise me that you (hasn't, haven't).
5.   She (hasn't, haven't) set any world records.
6.   She (doesn't, don't) claim to be a great artist.
7.   Raccoon (isn't, aren't) an Oscar winner.
8.   She and her friends (hasn't, haven't) been written up in popular magazines.
9.   She (wasn't, weren't) a star in the last Olympic games.
10.   (Aren't, Isn't) there millions of people just like Raccoon?
11.   I hope you (doesn't, don't) agree with the sentence above.
12.   A person (doesn't, don't) have to be famous to be unique.
13.   There (isn't, aren't) anyone in the world just like Raccoon.
14.   Raccoon and her friends (hasn't, haven't) led dull lives.
15.   Their adventures (hasn't, haven't) been written about, but maybe they should be.
16.   By the way, I (hasn't, haven't) told you that her family is from Transylvania.
17.   (Doesn't, Don't) be too sure that they (isn't, aren't) related to Prince Vlad.
18.   (Doesn't, Don't) that name mean something to you?
19.   (Wasn't, Weren't) Prince Vlad the real name of Count Dracula?
20.   Prince Vlad (wasn't, weren't) a nice person, to put it mildly.
21.   Raccoon (isn't, aren't) sure she wants to find out whether she really is related to Prince Vlad.

PART II   Write sentences using the contractions in parentheses. (Score: 2)

22.   (aren't)   _____

23.   (doesn't)   _____

Word Whiz   _____

Use the clues on the left to help you complete the words on the right. Use a dictionary for spelling help.

saying what something means
in another language   t r a n s __ __ __ i o n
giving blood to someone   t r a n s __ __ i o n
ways of moving people   t r a n s __ __ __ __ __ i o n

LESSON 82
Identifying Direct Objects—Nouns

Handbook Guides 45d, 45g, 45h

The direct object is the word that receives the action of a verb.

PART I In each sentence, draw one line under the verb or verb phrase that is the simple predicate. Draw two lines under the direct object. (Score: 46)

Example: Ralf Hotchkiss <u>has built</u> a better <u><u>wheelchair</u></u>.

1. As a teenager, Ralf Hotchkiss crashed his motorcycle.
2. Ever since, he has ridden a wheelchair.
3. In the sixties and seventies, bulky wheelchairs caused problems for riders.
4. Hotchkiss wanted greater mobility.
5. At age 19, he built his first wheelchair.
6. It could climb stairs!
7. Today Hotchkiss designs wheelchairs for people throughout the world.
8. He also has designed airplanes.
9. In some ways, wheelchairs present a greater challenge.
10. All pilots fly airplanes in open skies.
11. Each wheelchair rider travels different paths.
12. Colleagues admire Hotchkiss's inexpensive, adaptable designs.
13. This talented designer also builds chairs himself.
14. He has arranged his workshop perfectly.
15. Pulleys hold equipment within easy reach.
16. Hotchkiss loves his work.
17. He never patents his designs.
18. That way, anyone can use them for free.
19. Hotchkiss founded the Whirlwind Wheelchair Network in 1980.
20. This organization helps riders in developing countries.
21. Wheelchair riders build chairs for themselves and others.
22. Hotchkiss's wheelchairs provide considerable independence.
23. In 1995, Hotchkiss won the Chrysler Award for innovation in design.

PART II Write two sentences of your own about a person who has built or made something. Each sentence should include a direct object. Circle the direct object in each sentence. (Score: 6—3 for each sentence)

24. _____

     _____

25. _____

     _____

Name_____   Perfect Score 64   My Score _____

LESSON 83
Identifying Predicate Nouns and Predicate Adjectives

> **Handbook Guide 45i**
>
> **A predicate noun follows a linking verb and renames the subject. A predicate adjective follows a linking verb and describes the subject.**

PART I   Draw one line under the simple subject in each sentence. Draw two lines under the simple predicate. Circle each predicate noun and each predicate adjective. On the line write whether the word you circled is a predicate noun or a predicate adjective. (Score: 60)

Example:

American <u>cities</u> <u>are</u> often (noisy.)_____ *predicate adjective*
A <u>garden</u> <u>can be</u> a restful (place.)_____ *predicate noun*

1.   Traffic is heavy in downtown San Francisco. _____
2.   Sidewalks are crowded throughout the day. _____
3.   With its many tall buildings, the city can seem cold. _____
4.   Chinatown is a neighborhood in the downtown area. _____
5.   Portsmouth Square is a park in this neighborhood. _____
6.   It is an island of green. _____
7.   The park is popular with residents and workers. _____
8.   Warren Suen is a native of San Francisco. _____
9.   Chinatown has always been his home. _____
10.   During World War II he was a member of the United States Navy. _____
11.   After the war he became a gardener for the city. _____
12.   In the opinion of many, this job is difficult. _____
13.   Care of flowers, trees, and lawns is a test of stamina. _____
14.   Clean-up and maintenance are time-consuming. _____
15.   The work can seem endless. _____
16.   Warren Suen was the gardener at Portsmouth Square for thirty years. _____
17.   He was a skillful caretaker of all the plants. _____
18.   He was also a friend to the park's regular visitors. _____
19.   Thanks to his kindness, many residents felt less lonely. _____
20.   In the words of Jenny Lew, a community leader, Warren Suen is an unsung hero.

_____

PART II   Write two sentences about an unsung hero you know. Use a predicate noun in one sentence and a predicate adjective in the other. (Score: 4—2 for each sentence)

_____
_____
_____
_____

LESSON 84
Identifying Troublesome Words and
Expressions

PART I   Underline the proper word or expression in parentheses. (Score: 19)

1.   The harbor area of Baltimore (has, has got) many interesting places to visit.
2.   You (should have, should of) been there last Monday.
3.   The Baltimore Orioles baseball team (must of, must have) been playing at Camden Yards, their home field.
4.   Baltimore (has, has got) a long history and a strong identity.
5.   You (must of, must have) (heard, heered) about the battle that inspired "The Star-Spangled Banner."
6.   You (might not have, might not of) realized that it was fought in Baltimore.
7.   It seemed as if there wasn't (any, no) chance that the Americans could keep the British from capturing the city.
8.   The American forces (must of, must have) fought fiercely because they defeated the British in that battle.
9.   Baltimore (growed, grew) into a large industrial city during the 1800s.
10. The city (drawed, drew) immigrants from Germany, Ireland, Italy, Poland, and elsewhere.
11. (Haven't, Ain't) you read (any, none) of Edgar Allan Poe's stories?
12. He (written, wrote) many of his tales in a row house on Amity Street.
13. Babe Ruth, the great home run hitter, (grew, growed) up in an orphanage in Baltimore.
14. Have you (heard, heered) about what he did for the game of baseball?
15. Baltimore also (has got, has) one of the finest hospitals in the United States.
16. You (must of, must have) (heered, heard) that it is a lively city.

PART II   Rewrite the following sentences properly. (Score: 3)

17. I should of knowed that the city was founded by Lord Baltimore. _____

_____

18. The city has got many elegant mansions. _____

_____

19. You couldn't of drug me away from the aquarium with a tow truck. _____

_____

Connecting Meanings _____

Draw a line from each word in row 1 to its meaning in row 2. Then write a sentence using each word in row 1.

Row 1	principal	principle	principality
Row 2	important rule	land ruled by a prince	person with authority

Name_____   Perfect Score 29   My Score _____

LESSON 85
Using Standard Forms

PART I   Underline the proper word in parentheses. (Score: 25)

1. (Their, They're, There) are many kinds of bread.

2. Bread (don't, doesn't) have to be made of wheat.

3. (Have, Has) you ever (eaten, ate) Scottish oatcakes or barley bannocks?

4. Freshly made corn tortillas (is, are) a real treat.

5. In Norway and Sweden, barley and rye (is, are) used in breads of many kinds.

6. (Them, Those) grains grow well (their, they're, there).

7. We (went, gone) to a Jamaican restaurant.

8. The owners made (their, they're, there) own coconut bread.

9. Lavash is a favorite of (ours, our's).

10. The rounds of this Armenian cracker bread (is, are) about two feet across!

11. Most of (we, us) San Franciscans have (ate, eaten) warm sourdough French bread.

12. Steamed buns (is, are) often served with Peking duck; these are called *bow*.

13. Have you ever (seen, saw) bagels being made?

14. (Their, They're, There) first boiled and then baked.

15. There (is, are) few breads thinner than matzo.

16. In some parts of the South a popular form of bread (is, are) corn pone.

17. (Doesn't, Don't) it taste just like corn bread?

18. Have you ever (ate, eaten) hush puppies?

19. There (is, are) several stories about how the hush puppy got (its, it's) name.

20. (Don't, Doesn't) it have something to do with the early range riders and settlers?

21. Did they throw bits of the bread to (their, they're, there) dogs to keep them quiet?

PART II   Write sentences using the words in parentheses. (Score: 4)

22. (themselves) _____

23. (became) _____

24. (were) _____

25. (learned) _____

UNIT VIII

LESSON 86
Capitalization and Punctuation

Handbook Guides 1c, 1e, 2a, 2b, 2f–h, 9, 11, 12, 13a, 14

PART I Underline each word that should begin with a capital letter. Add necessary punctuation marks. (Score: 77)

1. gail i don't even know what a hydrofoil is said lani

2. youll soon find out said gail

3. the two friends stood by the harbor of the city of charlotte amalie

4. beyond the harbor lay the caribbean sea

5. they were leaving st. thomas to visit gails relatives, the sánchezes, in san juan puerto rico

6. here comes the hydrofoil exclaimed gail

7. im not sure i want to ride in that said lani quietly

8. oh come on said gail

9. they stood in line walked forward and finally stepped aboard

10. its name is the *canaria* remarked gail

11. soon the *canaria* was cruising over the ocean surface

12. were traveling almost forty-five miles an hour a passenger said to lani

PART II Rewrite the following sentences, using proper capitalization and punctuation. (Score: 25—5 for each sentence written properly)

13. yes and were being propelled by two high-speed water jets added gail _____

   _____

14. she then explained that the hydrofoil has struts which reach down into the sea _____

   _____

15. afterwards lani said that the trip had been smooth quick and pleasant _____

   _____

16. gail said yes hydrofoils run smoothly even in six-foot waves _____

   _____

17. gail im really enjoying my caribbean vacation said lani _____

   _____

Name_____

LESSON 87
Writing a Story

Read a Story

Handbook Guides 18, 28

A story is one kind of narrative. Most stories include characters, a setting, and a plot invented by the author. The purpose of most stories is to entertain readers.

When you write a **story**, you invent characters, put them in a certain place and time, and then tell what happens to them. In a fiction story, the characters and events come from the writer's imagination. Here are some guidelines for writing a story:

- Make sure your story has a **beginning**, a **middle**, and an **end**.
- Introduce your **characters** at the beginning. Also reveal the **setting**—the time and place in which your story happens.
- Develop a **plot**. A plot often describes a **problem** one of the characters has, and then describes a **sequence of events** that leads to a **resolution** at the end.
- Choose a **voice** in which to tell the story. Stories are usually told in **third-person voice**. This means that the writer refers to characters using the pronouns *he*, *she*, and *they*.
- Use **dialogue**, the actual words spoken by characters, to make your story come alive.

Read this example of a story:

Trading Green for Green

For the third time in three days, Matt found himself standing in front of the picture window of Rossi's Sporting Goods, checking out the gleaming mountain bikes. He had his bike all picked out—the green one at the end of the row. Aaron, his best friend, agreed with his choice. "Man, that's a beauty," he said, admiring the bike. "But how're you going to get the money to buy it?"

"That's the question," Matt thought to himself as he and Aaron turned away from the window and headed up North Street. The hot Georgia sun beat down. Matt thought about how great it would be to ride that cool bike to the pool instead of waiting at the bus stop, roasting in the heat. So far, though, he'd only made one hundred forty-seven dollars, and it was already August. In a couple of weeks school would begin, and he'd have a lot less time for odd jobs. "I'll never get that bike," he muttered.

Aaron saw it first, a tiny glint on the gritty sidewalk. "Hey, what's that?" Aaron said, picking it up. Both boys stopped cold. It was a ring. A big beautiful gold ring with a huge green stone in the middle. "Think it's a fake?" Aaron asked as he turned the ring over and over.

Matt didn't know anything about jewelry, but somehow he knew that the ring in Aaron's hand was no fake. He tried to push the thought from his mind, but it kept coming back. The ring was probably worth a bundle of cash. They could sell it. "A green stone for a green bike," he murmured.

"Right you are," Aaron said, slapping him on the back. "And one for me, too!"

For the next few days, the ring stayed safe in Matt's bottom drawer, stuffed into a sock. Every now and then, when he was alone, he'd unroll the sock, take out the ring, and admire it. He'd never been to a pawn shop before, but he knew he could sell the ring at one. He even looked in the phone book and copied down the address of a pawn shop downtown. Another thought kept crowding into his mind, though. "Who is this ring's real owner?" he wondered. "Should I try to find her and return it?"

Finally his conscience won out. Four days after they found the ring, Matt called Aaron and told him he thought they should try to find the ring's real owner. Aaron was disappointed, but he agreed. The next day, Matt turned the ring in to Central Station. The police sergeant told Matt he'd done the right thing. "I know it," Matt thought to himself as he sat sweating in the sizzling heat at the bus stop, "but I'll never get that bike now."

Three days later a phone call came for Matt. It was the sergeant from Central Station. He said that the lady who owned the ring was so grateful it had been returned that she wanted to thank the person who found it. In the next day's mail, Matt got a letter from a woman named Mrs. Appleton. With it was a check for two hundred fifty dollars. Half of that plus the money Matt had already earned was just enough for that bright green bike.

Complete these items about the story.

1. Put a box around the names of the two most important **characters** in the story.

2. Circle a detail that tells **where** the story takes place. Put a box around one that shows **when**.

3. What was the **problem** in the story? Underline the sentences that reveal it.

4. Underline the sentences that show the **resolution**.

5. Put an X by each bit of **dialogue**.

Write a Story

Now it's your turn to write a story. The steps that follow will help you.

I. Prewriting

1. Think of a Story Idea. Use the characters and problems listed below to give you some ideas for your story. Think of other ideas, too.

Characters		Problems
a lost sailor	a famous ballerina	must escape from danger
two city boys	a lone hiker	must solve a mystery

2. Make a Story Map. On another sheet of paper, list your characters, setting, and plot.

II. Write a First Draft. Using your story map to help you, write a first draft on another piece of paper. Write your first draft quickly. Just try to get all your ideas down. You'll have a chance to revise and correct your writing later.

III. Revise. Read your first draft. Ask yourself these questions: Does it have a beginning, a middle, and an end? Have I included details about the setting? Is the sequence clear? Does the ending make sense? Have I used dialogue to make the story come alive and show what the characters are like? Then make revisions to your story.

IV. Proofread. Read over your revised story carefully. Look for errors in spelling, punctuation, and capitalization. Make sure you have punctuated dialogue correctly. Also make sure you begin a new paragraph with each change of speaker.

V. Publish. Make a clean copy of your story. Write it by hand, or type it using a word processor. Then share your story with a friend, family member, or teacher.

Name _____   Perfect Score 14   My Score _____

LESSON 88
Unit VIII Review

1. Combine each pair of sentences below, using the connecting word *and*. (Score: 3)   Handbook Guides 24a, 24b

   Jodie Foster is a fine actress. She is also a noted director and producer.

   _____

   _____

   She has been acting since she was two years old. She has appeared in many movies.

   _____

   _____

   She attended Yale University. She graduated with highest honors in 1985.

   _____

   _____

2. Combine each pair of sentences below, using a connecting word other than *and*. (Score: 2)   Handbook Guides 24a, 24c

   Her desk is clean. My desk is cleaner.

   _____

   I've worked the hardest. I deserve the award.

   _____

3. Rewrite the words below, placing hyphens between the syllables. Use a dictionary to help you. (Score: 6)   Handbook Guide 44

   commanding _____   rolling _____

   tossing _____   swimming _____

   canning _____   suffering _____

4. On the lines below write a short paragraph about a movie, TV program, or story you have enjoyed recently. Underline two adjectives you use. Circle two adverbs you use. (Score: 5)   Handbook Guides 22–24, 28

   _____

   _____

   _____

   _____

   _____

LESSON 89
Reviewing Sentences

PART I   Write the word *yes* before each group of words that is a sentence and the word *no* before each group that is not a sentence. Place the appropriate end punctuation mark after each sentence. (Score: 18)

_____   1.   Luther Burbank, a famous American plant breeder

_____   2.   Born on March 7, 1849, in Lancaster, Massachusetts

_____   3.   As a child he was interested in plants and gardening

_____   4.   Liked to experiment with many kinds of plants

_____   5.   The Burbank potato from seedlings

_____   6.   In 1875 Burbank moved to California

_____   7.   Didn't he develop the Shasta daisy there

_____   8.   Named for a mountain peak in California

_____   9.   Later Burbank developed the white blackberry

_____   10.   What a funny name that is for a berry

_____   11.   The berry is so clear that you can see the seeds inside it

_____   12.   Many very important contributions to agriculture

PART II   Add words and punctuation to the following word groups to make sentences. (Score: 9—3 for each sentence)

13.   (large tomato plants)   _____

_____

14.   (growing vegetables behind our apartment building)   _____

_____

_____

15.   (delicious home-grown potatoes)   _____

_____

_____

Optional Exercise: Consult reference books to learn about other interesting discoveries of Luther Burbank. Write a short paragraph telling about them.

LESSON 90
Reviewing the Business Letter

On the lines below write a business letter, following the instructions in one of the two numbered paragraphs. In your letter, use abbreviations where it is appropriate to do so. Be sure to include all parts of the business letter and to place them properly. Use your own address in the heading. (Score: 30—5 for each part of the letter written correctly)

(1) All-Truck Parts Company (located at 1357 North Industrial Street, Chicago, Illinois 60607) sells truck parts by mail. The company states that in this way it can sell the parts more cheaply. Write to the company, asking the price of a new tire for a 1998 Haulmore truck.

(2) All-Seasons Fashions (located at 495 Flatbush Avenue, Brooklyn, New York 11238) is advertising that it sells clothing by mail at a cheaper price. Write to the company, asking for a catalogue and an order blank. Also ask if the clothing can be exchanged if it is the wrong size.

_____

_____

_____

_____

_____

_____

_____

_____

_____

_____

_____

_____

_____

Odd Word Out _____

Circle the word in this list that does not belong with the others. Name a category that would fit the four uncircled words. Then name a category for the word you circled.

tugboat   locomotive   clipper   supertanker   galleon

LESSON 91
Reviewing Plurals, Possessives, and Contractions

Handbook Guides 14, 16, 17

PART I Write the plural forms of the following words. (Score: 14)

1. firefighter _____
2. child _____
3. self _____
4. chimney _____
5. dog _____
6. match _____
7. man _____

8. mouse _____
9. foot _____
10. calf _____
11. rally _____
12. ox _____
13. wharf _____
14. attorney _____

PART II Write the possessive forms of the following words. (Score: 14)

15. Mrs. Hawkins _____
16. Lois _____
17. Richard _____
18. class _____
19. women _____
20. Americans _____
21. classes _____

22. horse _____
23. soldiers _____
24. Ross _____
25. entry _____
26. kitten _____
27. people _____
28. Kelly _____

PART III Write the contractions of the following words. (Score: 14)

29. we have _____
30. you have _____
31. she is _____
32. cannot _____
33. does not _____
34. I will _____
35. are not _____

36. they are _____
37. will not _____
38. should not _____
39. that is _____
40. you are _____
41. could not _____
42. do not _____

Name_____   Perfect Score 57   My Score _____

LESSON 92
Reviewing Direct and Indirect Quotations

PART I   Punctuate the following direct and indirect quotations. (Score: 37)

1. What's that machine in your back yard asked Al

2. That's an oil well said Dolores

3. No, really, what is it asked Al

4. Dolores told him she was telling the truth

5. I thought oil wells were huge said Al

6. Dolores explained that small oil wells are quite common

7. In fact, more than three quarters of the oil wells in the United States are small she said

8. Is there a special name for a small oil well asked Al

9. Dolores said A well that produces less than ten barrels a day is called a stripper

10. Then she said that more than 400,000 wells in the U.S. are strippers

11. Al asked Does your family make much money from your well's production

12. Dolores told Al that they did

13. Al said that he wouldn't mind having an oil well in his back yard

PART II   Rewrite the following indirect quotations as direct quotations. Add all necessary punctuation and capitalization. (Score: 20—4 for each sentence)

14. Then Al said that maybe he should drill there. _____

_____

15. Dolores said that drilling there probably wasn't a good idea. _____

_____

16. She said that drilling for oil is very expensive. _____

_____

17. Al asked when Dolores's well had been drilled. _____

_____

18. She said that her grandparents had drilled it many years ago. _____

_____

LESSON 93
Reviewing Homophones, Synonyms, and Antonyms

PART I   Underline the proper word in parentheses. (Score: 10)

1. Do you (no, know) much about our forty-ninth state?

2. I (heard, herd) that (their, there) are volcanoes in Alaska.

3. If (your, you're) fortunate you may (sea, see) one of them.

4. The midnight sun (shone, shown) brightly this June in Atkasook and Kaktovik.

5. (Its, It's) a beautiful place, especially when the skies are (blew, blue).

6. I am going (to, too, two) Alaska (one, won) day.

PART II   Write a sentence using a synonym of each word in parentheses. (Score: 8)

7. (slice) _____

8. (large) _____

9. (grumpy) _____

10. (remain) _____

11. (choose) _____

12. (allow) _____

13. (grinning) _____

14. (gift) _____

PART III   Write a sentence using an antonym of each word in parentheses. (Score: 8)

15. (stale) _____

16. (inside) _____

17. (new) _____

18. (slow) _____

19. (friend) _____

20. (often) _____

21. (shut) _____

22. (win) _____

Name _____   Perfect Score 22   My Score _____

LESSON 94
Reviewing Standard Verb Forms

Handbook Guides 20a, 20b, 21, 33, 34, 36, 37, 39, 41

PART I   Underline the correct verb form in parentheses. (Score: 13)

1. Carlos Ochoa (is, are) a treasure hunter.
2. It has (took, taken) Ochoa years to find rare Incan treasures.
3. The treasures (is, are) not jewels, gold, and silver.
4. He has (went, gone) all through the Andes searching for potatoes.
5. Tribes in the Andes (has, have) raised potatoes for nearly two thousand years.
6. Before 1550 there (wasn't, weren't) any potatoes in Europe.
7. Potato growing (began, begun) after Spanish explorers brought home the plants.
8. The potato did not (come, came) to North America until 1621.
9. These vegetables (is, are) now grown in every state.
10. You probably have (saw, seen) four or five different kinds.
11. For many years there (wasn't, weren't) any real interest in other potato varieties.
12. Many types (could have, could of) died out, if it weren't for Carlos Ochoa.
13. What he has (did, done) is collect native potato varieties.

PART II   Write a sentence using each word in parentheses. (Score: 9)

14. (don't)   _____
15. (may)   _____
16. (lie)   _____
17. (laid)   _____
18. (lain)   _____
19. (sat)   _____
20. (set)   _____
21. (give)   _____
22. (learned) _____

Word Whiz _____

Use the clues on the left to help you complete the words on the right. Use a dictionary for spelling help.

helpful   __ __ __ __ f i c i a l

on the surface; not deep   __ __ __ __ __ f i c i a l

not real   __ __ __ f i c i a l

LESSON 95
Reviewing Pronouns

PART I Underline the correct pronoun in parentheses. (Score: 20)

1. Ardena talked to (we, us) about market research.
2. It was (she, her) who said that curious people make good researchers.
3. She told Medhi and (I, me) that she tries to find out what people like.
4. (He, Him) and (I, me) tested a new snack food.
5. Medhi and (I, me) hated it.
6. Ardena told (he and I, him and me) that she would choose strangers for the real test.
7. (She, Her) and her co-workers also search books for facts.
8. Was it (she, her) who told us where store managers place animal crackers?
9. (They, Them) usually place them on a low shelf.
10. They are too low for (we, us) older people to see easily.
11. Children see (they, them), though, and ask the grown-up with them if they may have a box.
12. It is children who like (they, them) the most.
13. Companies can often use information to cause (we, us) to buy more.
14. Medhi plans to open an ice cream parlor by (hisself, himself).
15. It was (he, him) who asked Ardena to suggest a good location.
16. She asked (he, him) who he thought would be his best customers.
17. Medhi thought (they, them) would be young people.
18. "Open your parlor where (they, them) will pass it often," Ardena said.
19. So (Medhi and I, I and Medhi) spent days finding out what streets young people walk along often.

PART II Write sentences using the phrases in parentheses. (Score: 6)

20. (her and me)   _____
21. (it was he)   _____
22. (he and I)   _____
23. (us students)   _____
24. (between you and me) _____
25. (we friends)   _____

Name_____   Perfect Score 42   My Score _____

LESSON 96
Alphabetical Order and Word Division

In column 1 arrange the listed words in alphabetical order. In column 2 divide the alphabetized words into syllables.

		Column 1	Column 2
elbow	1.		
express	2.		
welcoming	3.		
balance	4.		
shopping	5.		
mistake	6.		
beginning	7.		
toadstool	8.		
before	9.		
unwilling	10.		
missing	11.		
legally	12.		
excellent	13.		
advise	14.		
hurrying	15.		
justice	16.		
finally	17.		
planning	18.		
misspell	19.		
describe	20.		
occurring	21.		

LESSON 97
Capitalization and Punctuation

PART I   Underline each word that should begin with a capital letter. Add necessary punctuation marks. (Score: 68)

1.   im tired of watching the same old programs on TV said jolene loudly

2.   well why dont you listen to the radio with me tonight asked leon

3.   you mean just sit around and listen to rock asked jolene disgustedly

4.   no im talking about listening to old radio shows said leon

5.   he explained that one station was playing nothing but shows from the old days

6.   she asked if he meant programs like the green hornet

7.   yes thats right leon answered

8.   old radio shows are funnier scarier and more interesting than TV shows he continued

9.   why do you think so asked jolene

10.   you can use your imagination to picture things you hear leon said

11.   jolene said that she herself had a pretty wild imagination

PART II   Rewrite the following sentences using appropriate capitalization and punctuation. (Score: 25—5 for each sentence)

12.   were in for some thrills on wednesday january 6 2000 said leon _____

_____

13.   jolene asked what show would be on that night _____

_____

14.   leon said that the show called richard diamond, private detective would be on _____

_____

15.   weren't dick powell ed begley and virginia gregg in that she asked _____

_____

16.   jolene you know more about old-time radio than i do leon said _____

_____

UNIT IX

Name_____   Perfect Score 96   My Score _____

LESSON 98
Unit IX Review

1. Write the word *yes* before each group of words that is   Handbook Guides 1a, 1c
    a sentence and the word *no* before each group of
    words that is not a sentence. Place the appropriate end punctuation mark after each
    sentence. (Score: 7)

    _____ Indiana, the smallest state in the Midwest

    _____ Hiking on the famous sand dunes along Lake Michigan

    _____ Indiana residents often refer to themselves as Hoosiers

    _____ "The Crossroads of America" is the state motto

    _____ Indiana resident Jim Davis, the creator of the comic strip "Garfield"

2. Rewrite the sentences below, adding punctuation   Handbook Guides 1b–d, 2a, 2b, 2d, 2g,
    marks and capital letters. (Score: 39)   2h, 7d, 8, 9, 10a, 10c, 12, 13a, 14, 17b

    wasnt bret harte born in albany new york on august 25 1839 asked josh _____

    _____

    yes this early american author liked to write about gamblers adventurers and miners

    said sue _____

    _____

    then sue said that the luck of roaring camp was her favorite short story _____

    _____

    josé said that many of hartes story titles include the names of mining camps in california

    _____

    _____

3. Underline the proper form in parentheses. (Score: 4)   Handbook Guides 21, 33, 34, 36, 37

    May I (set, sit) on your new sofa?

    In order to (learn, teach) us yoga, the instructor had us (lie, lay) on our backs.

    (Doesn't, Don't) you want to try?

4. Alphabetize the words below. Then write a synonym   Handbook Guides 26, 27, 43a
    and an antonym for each word. (Score: 9)

	Synonym	Antonym
below	_____	_____
victory	_____	_____
modern	_____	_____

5. Write the plural forms of the following words.
   (Score: 10)

child	_____	berry	_____
chimney	_____	woman	_____
scarf	_____	moose	_____
foot	_____	flash	_____
latch	_____	shelf	_____

6. Write the possessive forms of the following words.
   (Score: 6)

Handbook Guide 17

soldier	_____	Evelyn	_____
man	_____	Patriots	_____
doctors	_____	monkey	_____

7. Write the contractions of the following words.
   (Score: 8)

Handbook Guide 14

you are	_____	I will	_____
we have	_____	they are	_____
it is	_____	cannot	_____
are not	_____	will not	_____

8. Write a homophone for each of the following words.
   (Score: 8)

Handbook Guide 25

shone	_____	mane	_____
to	_____	tale	_____
for	_____	wail	_____
weight	_____	you're	_____

9. Underline the correct pronoun in parentheses.
   (Score: 5)

Handbook Guides 18, 45h

Eddie and (I, me) are taking a test on Saturday.

It was (him, he) who suggested that we work for the United States Post Office.

A supervisor talked with (we, us) about jobs and requirements.

She encouraged (he and I, him and me) to take the examination.

We thanked (her, she) for the information and encouragement.

THE HANDBOOK

The Guide numbers on the lesson pages refer you to the information given in the following pages. There are forty-five Guides, many of which are divided into sections. The Guides contain rules, explanations, examples, and practice exercises.

Use the Guides whenever you need help with grammar, word use, capitalization, or punctuation. The Guides are listed by topic in alphabetical order at the end of this book.

Sentences

Guide 1a **A sentence is a group of words that expresses a complete thought.**

Our geology class is studying fossils.
Have you seen a dinosaur egg?
Yes, what an interesting fossil it was!

The following groups of words are not sentences. They do not express complete thoughts. They leave the reader expecting something else to be added.

The paintings in the gallery
When you visited the museum

Each of the word groups above can be made into a sentence by adding words that complete the thought.

The paintings in the gallery were old masterpieces.
Did you see the sword collection when you visited the museum?

Practice: Write the word *yes* before each group of words that is a sentence and the word *no* before each group that is not a sentence.

_____   1.   When it began to snow.

_____   2.   The trains by the station.

_____   3.   The taxis in the streets.

_____   4.   Everyone began to cheer.

_____   5.   The snow was cleared from the tracks.

Guide 1b **Begin the first word of a sentence with a capital letter.**

Rick and I spent the day at the airport.
Isn't it exciting to watch the jets take off?

Practice: Rewrite each sentence below, capitalizing the first word of each sentence.

1. this is a beautiful day. _____

2. the sun is shining brightly. _____

3. mac wants to go to the beach. _____

Guide 1c   **A statement is a sentence that tells something. It is also called a declarative sentence. Place a period after a statement or declarative sentence.**

Our club has a new project this year.

We are collecting toys for the "Toys for Tots" drive.

Practice: Place the correct punctuation mark after each statement below.

1. The club members began collecting toys just before the holidays

2. We have been given many new toys

3. The old toys will be repaired by the members

Guide 1d   **A question is a sentence that asks something. It is also called an interrogative sentence. Place a question mark after a question or interrogative sentence.**

When does your vacation begin?

Are you going to the game next Friday night?

Practice: Place the correct punctuation mark after each question below.

1. What is the correct time

2. Do you have a shop class today

3. Why were you late for the meeting

Guide 1e   **An exclamatory sentence is a sentence that expresses strong or sudden feeling. Place an exclamation point after an exclamatory sentence.**

Block that kick!

How beautiful the city looks in the moonlight!

Practice: Place the correct punctuation mark after each exclamatory expression and sentence below.

1. Hooray We've won the championship

2. Who is the girl in the red coat

3. What a beautiful dive that girl made

4. Follow that car

HANDBOOK

Guide 1a

1. no   2. no   3. no
4. yes   5. yes

Guide 1b

1. This is a beautiful day.
2. The sun is shining brightly.
3. Mac wants to go to the beach.

Guide 1c

1. The club members began collecting toys just before the holidays.
2. We have been given many new toys.
3. The old toys will be repaired by the members.

Guide 1d

1. What is the correct time?
2. Do you have a shop class today?
3. Why were you late for the meeting?

Guide 1e

1. Hooray! We've won the championship!
2. (not an exclamatory sentence)
3. What a beautiful dive!
4. Follow that car!

Capitalization

Guide 2a — Begin the first word in a sentence with a capital letter.

Please mow the lawn.

Practice: Rewrite each sentence below, capitalizing the first word of the sentence.

1. what is the weather forecast for tomorrow? _____

2. the paper says it will be sunny. _____

3. oh, how we need rain! _____

Guide 2b — Capitalize the names of persons and particular places and things (called proper nouns).

Amy Tan	Main Street	Washington Monument
Queen Elizabeth II	Missouri River	Bill of Rights
California	Hudson College	Grand Canyon
Texas	St. Paul's Church	United States Congress
Sioux City	John's Market	Rio de Janeiro

Practice: Write the following proper nouns correctly.

1. dolores cruz _____
2. los angeles _____
3. joan of arc _____
4. howard building _____

5. rose bowl _____
6. fifth avenue _____
7. jefferson memorial _____
8. yellowstone national park _____

Guide 2c — Capitalize the names of the days of the week.

Tuesday

Practice: Write the names of the days of the week.

1. _____   4. _____   6. _____

2. _____   5. _____   7. _____

3. _____

Guide 2d **Capitalize the months of the year. Do not capitalize the seasons.**

February (month)   fall (season)

Practice: Write the names of the twelve months and the four seasons.

1. _____   7. _____   13. _____

2. _____   8. _____   14. _____

3. _____   9. _____   15. _____

4. _____   10. _____   16. _____

5. _____   11. _____

6. _____   12. _____

Guide 2e **Capitalize the names of holidays and special days.**

Thanksgiving   Arbor Day

Practice: Write the following names correctly.

1. labor day _____   4. ramadan _____

2. st. patrick's day _____   5. memorial day _____

3. yom kippur _____   6. presidents' day _____

Guide 2f **Capitalize the word _I_.**

I believe I have caught a cold.

Practice: Rewrite the following sentence correctly.

1. i am going if i can get a ride. _____

Guide 2g **Capitalize words formed from the names of places.**

American   Mexican   Italian   Scottish

Practice: Write the following words correctly.

1. puerto rican _____   4. spanish _____

2. alaskan _____   5. hawaiian _____

3. indian _____   6. swedish _____

| Guide 2h | Capitalize the first word in a direct quotation. |

Mary asked, "What would you like to do?"

"Let's go roller blading," Tara said.

Practice: Rewrite the following sentences. Capitalize the first word of each direct quotation.

1. Helen asked, "why are you leaving so early?" _____

_____

2. "something is wrong with my car," said Tina. _____

_____

Answers to Guide 2 Practice Exercises

Guide 2a
1. What is the weather forecast for tomorrow?
2. The paper says it will be sunny.
3. Oh, how we need rain!

Guide 2b
1. Dolores Cruz
2. Los Angeles
3. Joan of Arc
4. Howard Building
5. Rose Bowl
6. Fifth Avenue
7. Jefferson Memorial
8. Yellowstone National Park

Guide 2c
1. Sunday
2. Monday
3. Tuesday
4. Wednesday
5. Thursday
6. Friday
7. Saturday

Guide 2d
1. January
2. February
3. March
4. April
5. May
6. June
7. July
8. August
9. September
10. October
11. November
12. December
13. winter
14. spring
15. summer
16. fall or autumn

Guide 2e
1. Labor Day
2. St. Patrick's Day
3. Yom Kippur
4. Ramadan
5. Memorial Day
6. Presidents' Day

Guide 2f
1. I am going if I can get a ride.

Guide 2g
1. Puerto Rican
2. Alaskan
3. Indian
4. Spanish
5. Hawaiian
6. Swedish

Guide 2h
1. Helen asked, "Why are you leaving so early?"
2. "Something is wrong with my car," said Tina.

Capitalization with Punctuation
Initials of Names

Guide 3 Capitalize an initial used in place of a name. Place a period after the initial.

Elena A. Ruiz	J. H. Martinelli
H. Alan Zimmer	F. D. R.

Practice: Rewrite the following names correctly.

1. jeanne w ellis _____

2. paul l dietz _____

3. r thomas mingo _____

4. p b wittier _____

Answers to Guide 3 Practice Exercises

1. Jeanne W. Ellis   2. Paul L. Dietz   3. R. Thomas Mingo   4. P. B. Wittier

Titles with Names

Guide 4 Begin a title used before a name with a capital letter. Place a period after the title if it is abbreviated.

Mr. Tom King (Mr. is the abbreviation for Mister.)

Mrs. Olivia King (Mrs. is the abbreviation for Mistress, the title of respect given to a married woman.)

Dr. Kim King (Dr. is the abbreviation for Doctor.)

Miss Anne King (Miss is the title given to an unmarried girl or woman. It has no abbreviation.)

Ms. LaShonda King (Ms. is a title that may be used for both married and unmarried women. It is followed by a period.)

Some other common titles used before names are listed below. For each title that can be abbreviated, the abbreviation is given in parentheses.

President (Pres.)	Reverend (Rev.)
Governor (Gov.)	Judge
Senator (Sen.)	Rabbi
Representative (Rep.)	Professor (Prof.)
Mayor	Lieutenant (Lt.)
Bishop	Sergeant (Sgt.)

Practice: Rewrite each of the following names correctly. If the title of respect can be abbreviated, use the abbreviation.

1. mister henry twelvetrees _____

2. reverend susan thomas _____

3. doctor pat simon _____

4. mayor kelley delano _____

5. mistress jane hunter _____

6. ms. trudy skyes _____

7. president john adams _____

8. judge hamid tabbah _____

Answers to Guide 4 Practice Exercises

1. Mr. Henry Twelvetrees
2. Rev. Susan Thomas
3. Dr. Pat Simon
4. Mayor Kelley Delano
5. Mrs. Jane Hunter
6. Ms. Trudy Skyes
7. Pres. John Adams
8. Judge Hamid Tabbah

Days of the Week

Guide 5   **Begin the abbreviation for the name of a day of the week with a capital letter. Place a period after the abbreviation.**

Sun. (Sunday)

Practice: Write the abbreviations for the days of the week.

1. _____   4. _____   7. _____

2. _____   5. _____

3. _____   6. _____

Answers to Guide 5 Practice Exercises

1. Sun.   2. Mon.   3. Tues.   4. Wed.   5. Thurs.   6. Fri.   7. Sat.

Months of the Year

Guide 6 Begin the abbreviation for a month of the year with a capital letter. Place a period after the abbreviation. May, June, and July are not usually abbreviated.

Jan. (January)

Practice: Write the abbreviations for the months of the year. If the name is not abbreviated, write the full name on the line.

1. _____ 5. _____ 9. _____

2. _____ 6. _____ 10. _____

3. _____ 7. _____ 11. _____

4. _____ 8. _____ 12. _____

Answers to Guide 6 Practice Exercises

1. Jan.   4. Apr.   7. July   10. Oct.
2. Feb.   5. May   8. Aug.   11. Nov.
3. Mar.   6. June   9. Sept.   12. Dec.

Addresses

Guide 7a In writing an address, capitalize the title and the name of the person, the name of the street, the name of the city, and both letters in the postal code abbreviation for the state.

Mr. Roger Robles
825 Elm Street
Saint Matthews, KY 40206

Practice: Rewrite the address below, using capital letters correctly.

1. dr. eleanor f. borden   _____

   1204 eagle blvd.   _____

   el paso, tx 79910   _____

HANDBOOK

Guide 7b — **In writing an address, place a comma between the name of the city and the postal code abbreviation for the state.**

Mr. Hans Reiner
1405 Lindsay Place, Apt. 7
Mason City, IA 50401

Practice: Rewrite the address below, adding capital letters and punctuation marks.

1. mrs jeremy burton   _____

   7221 san angelo drive   _____

   san bernardino ca 92402   _____

Guide 7c — **Begin with a capital letter each abbreviation used in an address. Place a period after the abbreviation unless it is written with two capital letters.**

Co. (Company)   Ave. (Avenue)   IL (Illinois)
E. (East)   Bldg. (Building)   KY (Kentucky)
N. (North)   Blvd. (Boulevard)   MI (Michigan)
S. (South)   Dr. (Drive)   NY (New York)
W. (West)   St. (Street)   SD (South Dakota)
NW (Northwest)   AZ (Arizona)   TX (Texas)
SW (Southwest)   CO (Colorado)   VA (Virginia)

Practice: Rewrite the address below, using capital letters and punctuation marks correctly.

1. ms c m phillips   _____

   1305 s w county dr   _____

   lansing mi 48924   _____

Guide 7d — **When part or all of an address is written in a sentence, place commas as follows: after the name of the person or company, after the street address or box number, after the city, and after the state or territory, or zip code. If the address comes at the end of a sentence, use the correct end punctuation mark at the end of the sentence.**

Joe Murdock lives in Trenton, New Jersey, doesn't he?

Have you ever visited Boston, Massachusetts?

San Juan, Puerto Rico, is about a thousand miles from Florida.

Will you address this envelope to Jones-Simpson Company, Box 2242, Eugene, Oregon 97401?

Practice: Place commas and end punctuation marks correctly.

1. Dover Delaware is the state capital

2. Does Arturo live in Boulder Colorado

3. No, he lives in Billings Montana

4. Mail your application to Biloxi Box Company Box 14 Biloxi Mississippi 39530

Answers to Guide 7 Practice Exercises

Guide 7a
1. Dr. Eleanor F. Borden
   1204 Eagle Blvd.
   El Paso, TX 79910

Guide 7b
1. Mrs. Jeremy Burton
   7221 San Angelo Drive
   San Bernardino, CA 92402

Guide 7c
1. Ms. C. M. Phillips
   1305 SW County Dr.
   Lansing, MI 48924

Guide 7d
1. Dover, Delaware, is the state capital.
2. Does Arturo live in Boulder, Colorado?
3. No, he lives in Billings, Montana.
4. Mail your application to Biloxi Box Company, Box 14, Biloxi, Mississippi 39530.

Titles

Guide 8a   **Capitalize the first word and every important word in the title of a book, a story, a motion picture, a song, a report, and so on.**

   The Last of the Mohicans   Repairing a Generator

Such words as *a, an, the, of, for, in,* and *to* are usually not capitalized unless they begin or end a title. Verbs such as *is* and *are* are always capitalized in a title.

Practice: In the titles below, underline the words that should be capitalized.

1. a tale of two cities

2. the green hills of earth

3. apple is my sign

4. how to tune a car

Guide 8b Place quotation marks around the title of a poem, a short story, a song, or a TV or radio program when it is part of a sentence.

I thought "The Gold Bug" was an exciting story.

Practice: Place quotation marks around the titles in the sentences below.

1. The television show Roots traced a family from Africa to America.

2. I just read a ghost story called The Haunted Space Suit.

Guide 8c Draw a line under the title of a book, movie, album, magazine, or play when it is part of a sentence. If you are using a word processor, use italic type to write the name of a book, movie, album, magazine, or play.

I want to read <u>Paradise</u>.
or
I want to read *Paradise*.

Practice: Underline the titles in the sentences below.

1. Toy Story was a popular animated film.

2. The book I'm reading now is The Red Pony, by John Steinbeck.

Answers to Guide 8 Practice Exercises

Guide 8a
1. <u>a tale of two cities</u>
2. <u>the green hills of earth</u>
3. <u>apple is my sign</u>
4. <u>how to tune a car</u>

Guide 8b
1. The television show "Roots" traced a family from Africa to America.
2. I just read a ghost story called "The Haunted Space Suit."

Guide 8c
1. <u>Toy Story</u> was a popular animated film.
2. The book I'm reading now is <u>The Red Pony</u>, by John Steinbeck.

Guide 9a

A direct quotation tells the exact words of a speaker or writer. An indirect quotation gives the idea of the speaker or writer but does not give the exact words.

Chico said, "I need to buy some paper for my printer." (direct quotation)

Chico said that he needed to buy some paper for his printer. (indirect quotation)

Practice: Before each sentence write *D* if the sentence contains a direct quotation and *I* if the sentence contains an indirect quotation.

_____ 1. "Where are you going to buy the paper, Chico?" asked Marta.

_____ 2. Marta asked Chico where he was going to buy the paper.

_____ 3. Chico answered, "I'm going to the new store on Fourth Avenue."

_____ 4. Chico answered that he was going to the new store on Fourth Avenue.

Guide 9b

Place quotation marks around a direct quotation.

Kim asked, "Bill, where is your car?"

"I took it to the body shop," Bill replied.

Practice: Put quotation marks around the direct quotations.

1. What is the matter with your car? asked Kim.

2. It was in an accident, replied Bill.

3. Kim asked, How did it happen?

4. Bill said, Somebody backed into it.

Guide 9c

When the speaker's name comes before a direct quotation, place a comma before the beginning quotation marks. When the speaker's name comes after the direct quotation, place a comma, question mark, or exclamation point after the quotation, before the ending quotation marks.

Roy asked, "What are special effects?"

Dixie answered, "They are visual tricks used in motion pictures."

"Are special effects expensive to create?" asked Roy.

"Special equipment is often required," said Dixie.

"Look at that monster!" shouted Roy.

Practice: Add necessary punctuation marks to the sentences below.

1. Robert said "That is a beautiful sand painting."

2. Arthur asked "Will it be destroyed before nightfall?"

3. "That is our custom " answered Tocha.

4. "I've never seen anything so beautiful " cried Arthur.

5. "How are the colors made " asked Robert.

6. "The colors are made from powdered rock " said Tocha.

Guide 9d **Place the punctuation mark at the end of a direct quotation inside the quotation marks.**

Carl asked, "Did you see the parade yesterday?"

"Yes, I counted fifteen bands in the parade," said Maria.

"There must have been at least fifty floats!" exclaimed Dee.

Practice: In each sentence below, add the proper punctuation mark at the end of the direct quotation.

1. "One of the bands came from New Rochelle " said Carl.

2. "What a show " exclaimed Dee.

3. "Who were the people who carried the flags " asked Maria.

4. Dee replied, "That was the color guard "

5. Carl asked, "Did you see the drill team present arms "

6. Maria cried, "Oh, yes, they were very exciting "

Answers to Guide 9 Practice Exercises

Guide 9a
1. D   2. I   3. D   4. I

Guide 9b
1. "What is the matter with your car?" asked Kim.
2. "It was in an accident," replied Bill.
3. Kim asked, "How did it happen?"
4. Bill said, "Somebody backed into it."

Guide 9c
1. Robert said, "That is a beautiful sand painting."
2. Arthur asked, "Will it be destroyed before nightfall?"
3. "That is our custom," answered Tocha.
4. "I've never seen anything so beautiful!" cried Arthur.

5. "How are the colors made?" asked Robert.
6. "The colors are made from powdered rock," said Tocha.

Guide 9d
1. "One of the bands came from New Rochelle," said Carl.
2. "What a show!" exclaimed Dee.
3. "Who were the people who carried the flags?" asked Maria.
4. Dee replied, "That was the color guard."
5. Carl asked, "Did you see the drill team present arms?"
6. Maria cried, "Oh, yes, they were very exciting!"

Other Uses of Commas

Dates

Guide 10a **In writing a date, place a comma between the day of the month and the year. If no day is given, do not place a comma between the month and the year.**

January 1, 1997

January 1997

Practice: Place commas where needed in the dates below.

1. July 1776
2. March 14 1991
3. May 1812
4. September 16 1994
5. December 19 2003
6. June 20 1999

Guide 10b **In writing a date, place a comma between the day of the week and the month.**

Wednesday, October 26

Sunday, November 17, 2001

Practice: Place commas in the dates below.

1. Monday June 7
2. Tuesday May 5
3. Saturday September 10
4. Friday March 16 1866
5. Thursday April 12 1945
6. Wednesday September 24 1997

Guide 10c **When writing a date with month, day, and year in a sentence, place a comma after the year unless the year comes at the end of the sentence.**

On October 12, 1492, Columbus landed in the West Indies.

The First World War came to an end on November 11, 1918.

Practice: Add the correct punctuation mark after the year in the following sentences.

1. On June 6 1944 the Allies landed in France.

2. What important event took place on December 7, 1941

3. My brother was born in July 1994

4. On July 24 1997 my sister was born.

Answers to Guide 10 Practice Exercises

Guide 10a
1. July 1776
2. March 14, 1991
3. May 1812
4. September 16, 1994
5. December 19, 2003
6. June 20, 1999

Guide 10b
1. Monday, June 7
2. Tuesday, May 5
3. Saturday, September 10
4. Friday, March 16, 1866
5. Thursday, April 12, 1945
6. Wednesday, September 24, 1997

Guide 10c
1. On June 6, 1944, the Allies landed in France.
2. What important event took place on December 7, 1941?
3. My brother was born in July 1994.
4. On July 24, 1997, my sister was born.

Direct Address

<table>
<tr><td>**Guide 11**</td><td>**In writing a sentence, set off the name of a person whom you address by name (called direct address) with a comma or commas.**</td></tr>
</table>

Max, did you get a job?

May I leave work early today, *Ms. Ellis*?

If you need to leave early, *Francine*, you may.

Practice: In the sentences below, set off the names with commas.

1. Alex how are you feeling today?

2. I'm feeling better Diane.

3. If you want to go Danny please let me know.

Answers to Guide 11 Practice Exercises

1. Alex, how are you feeling today?
2. I'm feeling better, Diane.
3. If you want to go, Danny, please let me know.

Yes and No

<table>
<tr><td>**Guide 12**</td><td>**Place a comma after an introductory word such as *yes* or *no* at the beginning of a sentence or a direct quotation.**</td></tr>
</table>

Yes, I found my billfold.

No, the money was still inside it.

"*Well,* that was lucky," said Eric.

Practice: Place a comma after *yes* or *no* in the sentences below.

1. Yes I am going to the employment office today.

2. No I didn't make an appointment.

Answers to Guide 12 Practice Exercises

1. Yes, I am going to the employment office today.
2. No, I didn't make an appointment.

Words in a Series and Compound Sentences

Guide 13a **Use commas to separate words or phrases in a series. Place a comma before the conjunction in a series.**

Carol, Jim, Sally, and *I* are going to the hockey game.

Roberto left his *coat, hat,* and *jacket* in the locker.

The actor ran *out the door, down the steps,* and *across the stage.*

Practice: Add commas to each series in the sentences below.

1. The managers umpires and players entered the ball park.

2. I brought sandwiches fruit and sodas for the picnic.

3. Today Montie made a cake an apple pie and some cookies.

4. Carmen went to town bought a sandwich saw a movie and came home.

Guide 13b **Use a comma to separate the parts of a compound sentence. Place the comma before the word a*nd, but,* or *or* that joins the parts of the sentence.**

Kelvin washed the dishes, *and* Spud dried them.

Practice: In the sentences below, place commas where they are needed.

1. Karl wrote a book and David edited it.

2. It took them six months but finally they finished the book.

3. The book was published and many people enjoyed it.

Answers to Guide 13 Practice Exercises

Guide 13a
1. The managers, umpires, and players entered the ball park.
2. I brought sandwiches, fruit, and sodas for the picnic.
3. Today Montie made a cake, an apple pie, and some cookies.
4. Carmen went to town, bought a sandwich, saw a movie, and came home.

Guide 13b
1. Karl wrote a book, and David edited it.
2. It took them six months, but finally they finished the book.
3. The book was published, and many people enjoyed it.

Contraction

Guide 14 — A contraction is a word formed by combining a verb and the word *not*, or by combining a pronoun and a verb. In a contraction, one or more letters of the two words have been left out, and an apostrophe (') has been put in their place.

I haven't (have not) read the paper tonight.

She's (She is) the president of our club.

Below is a list of contractions and, in parentheses, the words from which each is formed.

1. isn't (is not)	15. shouldn't (should not)	29. you'd (you had)
2. aren't (are not)	16. I'm (I am)	30. he'd (he had)
3. wasn't (was not)	17. you're (you are)	31. she'd (she had)
4. weren't (were not)	18. he's (he is)	32. we'd (we had)
5. hasn't (has not)	19. she's (she is)	33. they'd (they had)
6. haven't (have not)	20. it's (it is)	34. I'll (I shall)
7. hadn't (had not)	21. that's (that is)	35. I'll (I will)
8. doesn't (does not)	22. we're (we are)	36. you'll (you will)
9. don't (do not)	23. they're (they are)	37. he'll (he will)
10. didn't (did not)	24. I've (I have)	38. she'll (she will)
11. won't (will not)	25. you've (you have)	39. we'll (we will)
12. wouldn't (would not)	26. we've (we have)	40. they'll (they will)
13. can't (cannot—can not)	27. they've (they have)	41. he'd (he would)
14. couldn't (could not)	28. I'd (I had)	42. they'd (they would)

The contraction *won't* is formed differently from other contractions. It is a contraction of the words *will not*.

Practice: Write the contraction of each word group listed below. Be sure to place the apostrophe correctly.

1. you have _____   4. do not _____

2. he will _____   5. I am _____

3. it is _____   6. you are _____

Answers to Guide 14 Practice Exercises

1. you've   2. he'll   3. it's   4. don't   5. I'm   6. you're

---

Nouns

Guide 15a	A noun names a person, a place, a thing, or an idea. A common noun is the general name of a person, place, or thing. A common noun is not capitalized unless it begins a sentence.

> woman (person)
>
> city (place)
>
> book (thing)

Practice: Underline the common nouns in the sentences below.

1. The server placed the chairs around the table.

2. The people took the subway to the park.

3. The traffic jammed the streets and bridges of the city.

Guide 15b	A proper noun is the particular name of a person, place, or thing. Begin a proper noun with a capital letter.

> Susan, Mr. Montanez (persons)   Colorado, Lake Erie (places)
>
> Grand Coulee Dam, Ronald Reagan Airport (things)

Practice: Underline the proper nouns in the sentences below.

1. Yachts from America and Australia took part in the race.

2. Diane and Liz spent a week in Newport.

3. They flew to La Guardia Airport in New York.

Answers to Guide 15 Practice Exercises

Guide 15a
The following words should be underlined:
1. server, chairs, table
2. people, subway, park
3. traffic, streets, bridges, city

Guide 15b
The following words should be underlined:
1. America, Australia
2. Diane, Liz, Newport
3. La Guardia Airport, New York

Singular and Plural Forms

Guide 16a   **A singular noun names one person, place, thing, or idea. A plural noun names more than one.**

Singular Nouns

engine

fruit

book

Plural Nouns

engines

fruits

books

Practice: Beside each noun write *S* if it is a singular noun and *P* if it is a plural noun.

1. hatch _____   3. rug _____   5. birds _____

2. curtains _____   4. cushion _____   6. pencils _____

Guide 16b   **The most common way to form the plural of a noun is to add the letter *s* to the singular form.**

picture   *pictures*   friend   *friends*

Practice: Write the plural form of each singular noun below by adding *s*.

1. pen _____   4. collector _____

2. paper _____   5. vacation _____

3. bank _____   6. material _____

Guide 16c   **To form the plural of a noun ending in *ch, sh, s,* or *x*, add *es* to the singular form.**

watch *watches*   mass *masses*

dish *dishes*   box *boxes*

Practice: Write the plural form of each of the following singular nouns by adding *es*.

1. scratch _____   3. loss _____

2. crash _____   4. wax _____

Guide 16d To form the plural of many nouns ending in *f* or *fe*, change the *f* or *fe* to *ve* and add *s*.

thief *thieves*   knife *knives*

Practice: Write the plural form of each of the following singular nouns by changing the *f* or *fe* to *ve* and adding *s*.

1. loaf _____   3. wife _____

2. half _____   4. life _____

Guide 16e To form the plural of a noun ending in a consonant and *y* (*by, dy, ly, my, ny, ry, ty,* and so on), change the *y* to *i* and add *es*.

army *armies*   baby *babies*

Practice: Write the plural form of each of the following singular nouns by changing the *y* to *i* and adding *es*.

1. pony _____   3. lady _____

2. lily _____   4. century _____

Guide 16f To form the plural of a noun ending in a vowel and *y* (*ay, ey, oy,* or *uy*), add *s*.

turkey *turkeys*   boy *boys*

Practice: Write the plural form of each of the following singular nouns by adding *s*.

1. day _____   3. toy _____

2. key _____   4. alloy _____

Guide 16g To form the plural of some nouns, change the spellings of the singular forms, or add a special ending.

goose *geese*   mouse *mice*

man *men*   ox *oxen*

Practice: Write the plural form of each of the following singular nouns:

1. woman _____   3. tooth _____

2. foot _____   4. child _____

Guide 16h The plural of some nouns is the same as the singular form.

deer   *deer*

fish   *fish* (sometimes written *fishes* in the plural)

Practice: Write the plural form of each of the following singular nouns.

1. sheep   _____   2. moose   _____

Answers to Guide 16 Practice Exercises

Guide 16a

1. S	3. S	5. P
2. P	4. S	6. P

Guide 16b

1. pens	4. collectors
2. papers	5. vacations
3. banks	6. materials

Guide 16c

1. scratches	3. losses
2. crashes	4. waxes

Guide 16d

1. loaves	3. wives
2. halves	4. lives

Guide 16e

1. ponies	3. ladies
2. lilies	4. centuries

Guide 16f

1. days	3. toys
2. keys	4. alloys

Guide 16g

1. women	3. teeth
2. feet	4. children

Guide 16h

1. sheep	2. moose *(or)* mooses

Possessive Forms

Guide 17a The possessive form of a noun shows ownership or possession.

That coat is *Ralph's*. (The coat is owned by or belongs to Ralph.)

The *store's* truck was stolen. (The truck is owned by or belongs to the store.)

Practice: Read each sentence in parentheses and answer the question after it.

1. (Belinda's sweater is red.) Who owns the sweater? _____

2. (The stranger's bag was on the train.) Who owns the bag? _____

3. (The book's cover is torn.) To what does the cover belong? _____

Guide 17b **To form the possessive of a singular noun, add an apostrophe and an s ('s).**

Eileen's sketch (the sketch drawn by Eileen)

The *team's* score (the score of the team)

Practice: Write the possessive form of each singular noun below.

1. jet   _____   3. cousin   _____

2. Sarah   _____   4. Chris   _____

Guide 17c **To form the possessive of a plural noun ending in s, add only an apostrophe (').
If the plural noun does not end in s, add an apostrophe and an s ('s).**

To decide which rule to follow in forming the possessive of a plural noun, first write the plural form of the noun and then add what is needed to make the plural form possessive.

girls' shoes (shoes belonging to girls)

men's hats (hats belonging to men)

Practice: Write the possessive form of each plural noun below.

1. sisters   _____   3. divers   _____

2. women   _____   4. officers   _____

Answers to Guide 17 Practice Exercises

Guide 17a
1. Belinda
2. the stranger
3. the book

Guide 17b
1. jet's
2. Sarah's
3. cousin's
4. Chris's

Guide 17c
1. sisters'
2. women's
3. divers'
4. officers'

Pronouns

Guide 18a	A pronoun is a word used in place of a noun. A personal pronoun takes the place of the name of a definite person or thing.

John is going with Bill and Mary. (nouns)

He is going with *him* and *her.* (pronouns)

Below is a list of personal pronouns used to take the place of nouns.

Subject Forms	*Object Forms*	*Possessive Forms*
I	me	my, mine
you	you	your, yours
he	him	his
she	her	her, hers
it	it	its
we	us	our, ours
they	them	their, theirs

Remember that *its* and *theirs* are pronouns and do not contain apostrophes, while *it's* and *there's* are contractions and do contain apostrophes.

Practice: Underline the pronouns in the sentences below.

1. The blue jacket is mine; the black one is hers.

2. When I have finished my lunch, I am going home.

3. Were you with him and her last night?

4. We saw them at the park.

5. They said that the keys were theirs.

Guide 18b	When a pronoun is the subject of the sentence, use one of the subject pronouns: *I, you, he, she, it, we,* or *they.*

She is a skillful performer.

They work at the radio station.

Practice: Underline the correct pronoun in parentheses.

1. (He, Him) and Jane are going to buy the groceries.

2. (She, Her) and Lisa visited the hospital.

3. (Them, They) are the girls who won the medals.

Guide 18c When a pronoun follows an action verb in a sentence, use one of the object pronouns: *me, you, him, her, it, us,* or *them*. They are called object pronouns because the word is usually the object of the action in the verb, or the object of a preposition.

Roy invited *me* to dinner.

We saw *him* and *them* at the diner.

Ellen told *him* and *us* to rest a while.

Practice: Underline the correct pronoun in parentheses.

1. Gina asked (she, her) to come to the party.

2. The boys have invited you and (I, me) to watch the rehearsal.

3. Karen sold Bill and (we, us) tickets to the play.

Guide 18d When a pronoun follows a preposition in a sentence, use one of the object pronouns: *me, you, him, her, it, us,* or *them*.

Will Dee go to the races with Luisa and *me?*

We received a postcard from *them*.

Give your order to *him* and *her*.

When using two or more pronouns after a preposition, decide which forms to use by reading the sentence with one pronoun at a time.

The records are for (*he* or *him*) and (*I* or *me*).

The records are for him (not *he*).

The records are for me (not *I*).

The records are for *him* and *me*.

Practice: Underline the correct pronoun in parentheses.

1. Between you and (I, me), I fell asleep during the movie.

2. The tennis match was won by George and (her, she).

3. We are going on the bus with (he, him) and (them, they).

Guide 18e After a form of the verb *to be* (*am, is, are, was,* or *were*), use a subject pronoun.

That is *he* in the red shirt.

The candidates are *he* and *she.*

It was *I* who called you last night.

Practice: Underline the correct pronoun in parentheses.

1. Was it (her, she) who won the election?

2. It was (I, me) who found the parking space.

3. The best skater is (she, her).

Guide 18f When using such expressions as *we boys* and *us girls,* remember that *we* is the subject pronoun and *us* is the object pronoun.

We serious runners don't mind a little rain.

The photographer took a picture of *us winners.*

Practice: Underline the correct pronoun in parentheses.

1. (We, Us) club members are planning a meeting.

2. The decision was made by (we, us) girls.

3. (We, Us) hockey players practice three hours a day.

4. Mr. Parker asked (we, us) poets to come up on stage.

Guide 18g When one or more nouns or pronouns are used with the pronoun *I* as the subject of a sentence, place the pronoun *I* last.

He and *I* are going to enter the golf match.

Felicia, Susan, and *I* are collecting for the United Fund.

Practice: Underline the proper word group in parentheses.

1. (Luis and I, I and Luis) are going fishing.

2. (I and he, He and I) want to catch some trout.

Guide 18h **When one or more nouns or pronouns are used with the pronoun *me* after an action verb or a preposition, place the pronoun *me* last.**

Mrs. Jenks sent *him* and *me* to buy a new record.

Pedro bought pizza for *Will, Nancy,* and *me.*

Practice: Underline the proper word group in parentheses.

1. Howard wants (me and Al, Al and me) to go to the gym.

2. The choice was between (Omar and me, me and Omar).

Guide 18i **The words *self* and *selves* may be combined with personal pronouns.**

Singular	*Plural*
myself	ourselves
yourself	yourselves
himself	themselves
herself	themselves
itself	themselves

Use *himself* or *themselves*, never *hisself* or *theirselves*.

Practice: Underline the proper word in parentheses.

1. Prince Alec (hisself, himself) attended the tennis match.

2. Ben and Lisa want to make the model airplane by (themselves, theirselves).

Answers to Guide 18 Practice Exercises

Guide 18a
The following words should be underlined:
1. mine, hers
2. I, my, I
3. you, him, her
4. We, them
5. They, theirs

Guide 18b
1. He   2. She   3. They

Guide 18c
1. her   2. me   3. us

Guide 18d
1. me   2. her   3. him, them

Guide 18e
1. she   2. I   3. she

Guide 18f
1. We   2. us   3. We   4. us

Guide 18g
1. Luis and I   2. He and I

Guide 18h
1. Al and me   2. Omar and me

Guide 18i
1. himself   2. themselves

Verbs

| Guide 19 | A verb shows action, being, or state of being. |

My dog *barked* at the hissing cat. (action)

Mrs. Thomas *is* the mayor of the city. (being)

This exercise *seems* difficult. (state of being)

Practice: Underline the verbs in the sentences below.

1. I bought a new CD today.

2. It is a collection of folk songs.

3. The singer was at the music store.

4. He autographed the CD for me.

5. He seemed very friendly.

6. Several people wanted the CD.

Answers to Guide 19 Practice Exercises

The following words should be underlined:
1. bought
2. is
3. was
4. autographed
5. seemed
6. wanted

With Singular Subjects and Plural Subjects

| Guide 20a | Use a singular verb with a singular subject noun. Use a plural verb with a plural subject noun or with two subject nouns. |

Singular

That *dog is* a beagle.

Our *neighbor has* a garden.

The *boy hasn't* any friends.

That *woman is* a lawyer.

Plural

Those *dogs are* beagles.

Our *neighbors have* gardens.

The *boys haven't* any friends.

That *man and woman are* lawyers.

Practice: Underline the proper verb in parentheses.

1. The banks (is, are) closed today.

2. In this state Lincoln's Birthday (is, are) a legal holiday.

3. Joe and Marta (has, have) a day off.

4. Usually they (goes, go) by subway to the park.

5. Mandy (is, are) still asleep.

6. (Isn't, Aren't) Michael at work on his car?

Guide 20b **Use a singular verb with a singular subject pronoun. Use a plural verb with a plural subject pronoun or with two subject pronouns.**

Singular	*Plural*
I am glad to see you.	*We are* glad to see you.
He drives well.	*They drive* well.
He isn't a pilot	*He and she aren't* pilots.

Practice: Underline the correct verb in parentheses.

1. They (is, are) basketball players.

2. He (wants, want) to join the Harlem Globetrotters.

3. He and she (has seen, have seen) their games on television.

4. It (takes, take) great skill to play on that team.

5. They (has traveled, have traveled) all over the world.

6. He (likes, like) to watch them tease their opponents.

Guide 20c **Use *are* or *were* (never *is* or *was*) with the pronoun *you*, whether it refers to one person or to more than one.**

You are my second cousin.

You are the girls who wrote the play.

Practice: Underline the correct verb in parentheses.

1. (Is, Are) you interested in skateboard racing?

2. I thought you (was, were) at the race last week.

3. Why (isn't, aren't) you at the race today?

Guide 20d Use *there is* or *there was* with a singular subject. Use *there are* or *there were* with a plural subject or with two singular subjects.

There is a good *picture* at the theater this week.

There are several *questions* on the test.

There were eighty passengers and five flight attendants on the airplane.

Practice: Underline the correct words in parentheses.

1. (There is, There are) my mother in the blue car.

2. (There was, There were) a loud clap of thunder.

3. (There is, There are) swarms of bees near that tree.

4. (There wasn't, There weren't) many boys at the soccer practice.

5. (There was, There were) three boys and a girl at the ticket window.

Answers to Guide 20 Practice Exercises

Guide 20a

1. are	2. is	3. have
4. go	5. is	6. Isn't

Guide 20b

1. are	2. wants	3. have seen
4. takes	5. have traveled	6. likes

Guide 20c

1. Are	2. were	3. aren't

Guide 20d

1. There is	2. There was
3. There are	4. There weren't
5. There were	

Principal Parts

Guide 21a	Verbs have three principal parts, the present form, the past form, and the past participle form.

Present	Past	Past Participle	Present	Past	Past Participle
become	became	become	begin	began	begun
blow	blew	blown	know	knew	known
break	broke	broken	lay	laid	laid
bring	brought	brought	learn	learned	learned
come	came	come	lie	lay	lain
do	did	done	raise	raised	raised
drag	dragged	dragged	ride	rode	ridden
draw	drew	drawn	rise	rose	risen
drink	drank	drunk	run	ran	run
drive	drove	driven	see	saw	seen
eat	ate	eaten	set	set	set
fly	flew	flown	sink	sank	sunk
freeze	froze	frozen	sit	sat	sat
give	gave	given	take	took	taken
go	went	gone	teach	taught	taught
grow	grew	grown	throw	threw	thrown
hear	heard	heard	write	wrote	written

Practice: Answer the questions below.

1. What is the past participle form of *blow?*   _____

2. What is the past form of *take?*   _____

3. What is the past form of *grow?*   _____

4. What is the past participle form of *hear?*   _____

5. What is the past participle form of *drag?*   _____

6. What is the past form of *bring?*   _____

Guide 21b The present form may stand alone, or it may have a helping verb such as *shall, will, can, may, do, does, did, should, could,* and *would.*

Without Helping Verbs
I *enjoy* swing dancing.
Shawn *plays* the drums.

With Helping Verbs
We *will* go to the street fair today.
Did you *see* my sunglasses?

Practice: Underline the helping verbs in the sentences below.

1. When can you leave for the game?

2. He will tell us about the TV schedule.

3. Do you have my motorcycle key?

4. Should I wait until you are ready?

Guide 21c   Do not use a helping verb with the past form.

Last night the water *froze* in the lake.
The leaky boat *sank* quickly.

Practice: Underline the correct verb in parentheses.

1. My sister (wrote, written) us a letter from Los Angeles.

2. Three months ago she (began, begun) her management training.

3. Everyone (went, gone) on long visits to the factory.

4. They also (did, done) many practice sales presentations.

5. One time my sister (saw, seen) a ten-mile-long traffic jam.

6. It (took, taken) her an hour to get past it.

Guide 21d With past participles always use one or more helping verbs such as *has, have, had, is, are, was, were,* and *been.*

I *have seen* that program several times.

Ardena *has* already *gone* home.

All the glasses in that shipment *could have* broken.

Practice: Underline the correct verb in parentheses.

1. I have (knew, known) Bianca for several years.

2. Willis has (went, gone) to get the tools we need.

3. The winning car was (drove, driven) by a mechanic.

4. I should have (wrote, written) to Ahmed.

5. We had already (saw, seen) what happened.

6. Have you ever (rode, ridden) a snowmobile?

Answers to Guide 21 Practice Exercises

Guide 21a

1. blown	2. took	3. grew
4. heard	5. dragged	6. brought

Guide 21b

The following words should be underlined:

1. can   2. will
3. Do   4. Should

Guide 21c

1. wrote   4. did
2. began   5. saw
3. went   6. took

Guide 21d

1. known	4. written
2. gone	5. seen
3. driven	6. ridden

Adjectives

Guide 22a	An adjective describes, or modifies, a noun or a pronoun. It tells what kind, how many, or which one.

George is reading an *exciting* novel. (tells what kind)

Colette has made *two* tables. (tells how many)

Brian sang the *first* song. (tells which one)

Practice: Underline the adjectives in the sentences below. (Do not underline the articles *a, an,* and *the.*)

1. We are walking through a famous square.

2. Do you see the two buildings over there?

3. One is a beautiful cathedral.

4. The other is an interesting museum.

5. The second building was once a prison.

6. Do you know the names of these buildings?

Guide 22b	The words *a, an,* and *the* are called articles. They also modify nouns. The article *a* is used before a word beginning with a consonant sound. The article *an* is used before a word beginning with a vowel sound.

the platypus   *a* horse   *an* octopus

Practice: Underline the correct article, *a* or *an,* in parentheses.

1. The restaurant has (a, an) good menu for today.

2. I stayed up late watching (a, an) old movie.

3. It was (a, an) adventure story about early Norwegian explorers.

4. One of them was (a, an) Viking called Eric the Red.

Answers to Guide 22 Practice Exercises

Guide 22a

The following words should be underlined:

1. famous	4. interesting
2. two	5. second
3. beautiful	6. these

Guide 22b

1. a
2. an
3. an
4. a

Adverbs

Guide 23 An adverb describes, or modifies, a verb, an adjective, or another adverb. It tells how, when, or where.

Anne sang *softly*. (tells *how*)

The boys left *yesterday*. (tells *when*)

He lives *here*. (tells *where*)

The meeting was *very* short. (tells *how* about an adjective)

She plays *quite* well. (tells *how* about another adverb)

Practice: Underline the adverbs in the following sentences.

1. Ms. Roberts spoke angrily.

2. He had arrived late.

3. Please put the wood there.

4. It was a terribly cold day.

Answers to Guide 23 Practice Exercises

The following words should be underlined:
1. angrily   2. late   3. there   4. terribly

Conjunctions

Guide 24a A coordinating conjunction is a word or phrase that connects words or groups of words in a sentence. Common conjunctions are *and, or, so,* and *but.*

Todd *and* Cecilia went to the amusement park.

Do you want cream *or* sugar?

Bing went fishing, *but* he didn't catch anything.

Practice: Underline the conjunctions in the sentences below.

1. My cousin and I went to the rodeo.

2. Did you prefer the roping contests or the trick riding?

3. We went to the stalls, but we couldn't see the horses.

Guide 24b Use conjunctions to combine short sentences into longer ones.

Eileen is a good speaker. Alberto is a good speaker.

Eileen *and* Alberto are good speakers.

Practice: On each line combine the two short sentences, using the conjunction *and.*

1. Ice hockey is a fast game. It is an exciting game.

_____

2. The game is played with curved sticks. It is played with a puck.

_____

3. The players wear padded uniforms. They wear shin guards.

_____

4. Hockey is popular in Canada. It is also popular in the United States.

_____

Guide 24c Other conjunctions often used in sentences are *when, until, where, which, because, as, after,* and *as soon as.* These words are called subordinating conjunctions. When a subordinate clause comes first in a sentence, use a comma after the clause. When a subordinate clause comes last, do not use a comma. Use these conjunctions to help indicate time, location, and relationships.

The girls went downtown. They saw a parade.

When the girls went downtown, they saw a parade.

Practice: Combine each of the following pairs of sentences into one sentence, using the conjunction in parentheses.

1. (when) My alarm clock rang. I did not get up. _____

_____

2. (because) I was late. I did not eat breakfast. _____

_____

3. (after) We left the stadium. We decided to get hamburgers. _____

_____

Answers to Guide 24 Practice Exercises

Guide 24a
The following words should be underlined:
1. and   2. or   3. but

Guide 24b
1. Ice hockey is a fast and exciting game.
2. The game is played with curved sticks and a puck.
3. The players wear padded uniforms and shin guards.
4. Hockey is popular in Canada and also in the United States.

Guide 24c
1. When my alarm clock rang, I did not get up.
2. Because I was late, I did not eat breakfast.
3. After we left the stadium, we decided to get hamburgers.

Word Study
Homophones

| **Guide 25** | Homophones are words that sound alike but have different spellings and different meanings. |

ate	Craig *ate* four hamburgers.	grease	There is *grease* in the pan.
eight	We need *eight* chairs.	Greece	Are you from *Greece*?
blew	The wind *blew* hard.	hear	I didn't *hear* you come in.
blue	Diane's eyes are *blue*.	here	Let's eat *here* at home.
buy	Did Kim *buy* a car?	heard	I *heard* a noise.
by	I was sitting *by* the door.	herd	We saw a *herd* of cattle.
cent	I don't have a *cent*.	hole	There is a *hole* in my sock.
sent	Lucas *sent* the package.	whole	My *whole* family is home.
dear	She is my *dear* friend.	it's	*It's* late!
deer	These *deer* are elands.	its	The cat licked *its* paws.
fair	We went to the street *fair*.	knot	Can you tie a square *knot*?
fare	What is the bus *fare*?	not	He does *not* want the job.
flour	This dough needs more *flour*.	knew	I *knew* you would win.
flower	That *flower* is an orchid.	new	This is a *new* tennis racket.
grate	The barbecue *grate* is hot.	know	I *know* the rules of hockey.
great	The lion gave a *great* roar.	no	We have *no* money.
meat	What kind of *meat* is that?	tail	The lynx has a short *tail*.
meet	Adele will *meet* us at four.	tale	This *tale* is about a clever coyote.
one	Let's play *one* more tape.	their	*Their* books were at home.
won	Max *won* the last game.	there	*There* is no more milk.
peace	I want *peace* and quiet.	they're	*They're* going to town.
piece	May I have a *piece* of cake?	threw	Phil *threw* the ball.
read	José has *read* that book.	through	He walked *through* the door.
red	I have a new *red* sweater.	to	Are you going *to* work?
read	Let's *read* this magazine.	too	I got here *too* late.
reed	Is that a *reed* whistle?	two	Sue bought *two* skirts.
rode	Yesterday I *rode* a horse.	weak	Tony was *weak* and ill.
rowed	Paddy *rowed* the canoe.	week	He will leave next *week*.
sea	The *sea* is quiet today.	who's	*Who's* going to town?
see	Do you *see* that ship?	whose	*Whose* apartment is that?
shone	The sun *shone* brightly.	wood	That *wood* is walnut.
shown	The movie was *shown* once.	would	*Would* you like to go?
son	He is Mrs. Fong's *son*.	you're	*You're* a good friend.
sun	The *sun* has set.	your	I found *your* pen.

Practice: Underline the correct word in parentheses.

1. Do you live (hear, here) or in the house across the street?

2. (It's, Its) too bad you don't live closer to my house.

3. How did those (to, too, two) people happen to (meat, meet)?

4. (Their, There, They're) are two robins nesting on our tree house.

5. I have a friend (whose, who's) going to school to learn welding.

6. When did you say (you're, your) leaving for vacation?

Answers to Guide 25 Practice Exercises

The following words should be underlined:
1. here   2. It's   3. two, meet   4. There   5. who's   6. you're

Synonyms

Guide 26   **Synonyms are words that have the same or nearly the same meaning.**

above—over	funny—amusing	save—rescue
afraid—frightened	get—obtain	short—brief
allow—let	gift—present	sick—ill
amazing—astonishing	hard—difficult	stay—remain
answer—reply	help—aid	still—quiet
antique—old	high—tall	story—tale
below—beneath	huge—enormous	strange—unusual
brave—courageous	hunt—search	talk—speech
buy—purchase	large—big	thin—slender
carton—box	lift—raise	think—believe
choose—select	orderly—neat	throw—toss
clumsy—awkward	piece—part	toil—labor
cry—weep	push—shove	trip—journey
cut—slice	real—genuine	tune—melody
dull—boring	rich—wealthy	under—beneath
foe—enemy	rude—impolite	within—inside

A thesaurus is a helpful reference work for finding synonyms.

Practice: Write a synonym for each word below.

1. below _____   3. afraid _____

2. huge _____   4. piece _____

Answers to Guide 26 Practice Exercises

1. beneath   2. enormous   3. frightened   4. part

Antonyms

| Guide 27 | **Antonyms are words that have opposite meanings.** |

above—under	high—low	rich—poor
add—subtract	idle—busy	right—wrong
antique—new	inside—outside	rise—fall
arrive—leave	large—small	rude—polite
back—front	laugh—cry	shiny—dull
before—after	loose—tight	shut—open
buy—sell	lose—win	slow—fast
cowardly—brave	loud—soft	stale—fresh
dark—light	many—few	stop—go
dull—sharp	mild—harsh	strong—weak
ending—beginning	new—old	thin—thick
foe—friend	often—seldom	throw—catch
full—empty	orderly—messy	top—bottom
frown—smile	over—under	true—false
graceful—awkward	pretty—ugly	up—down
grasp—drop	prompt—late	wild—tame
happiness—sadness	real—imitation	work—play

Practice: Write an antonym for each word below.

1. graceful _____   5. prompt _____

2. loud _____   6. real _____

3. stop _____   7. laugh _____

4. full _____   8. thick _____

Answers to Guide 27 Practice Exercises

1. awkward   2. soft   3. go   4. empty
5. late   6. imitation   7. cry   8. thin

Paragraphs

Guide 28a	A paragraph is a group of sentences that tells about one topic, or subject. A paragraph should begin with a sentence that introduces the topic of the paragraph.

Yesterday I started my first job. (topic sentence for a paragraph about a new job)

Practice: Read the paragraph below and then answer the questions about it.

A new bowling alley has just opened on Parker Avenue. It is the biggest alley I've ever seen. There are fifty pairs of bowling lanes, each with its own scoring machine, chairs for the players and friends, and a soft-drink machine. At one end of the alley is a restaurant. There are small-sized lanes and computer games for children. There is even a supervised play area for toddlers. It will be fun to bowl at this beautiful new alley.

1. What is the topic of the paragraph? _____

2. What does it tell about this topic? _____

Guide 28b	In writing a paragraph, follow the suggestions below.

- If the paragraph has a title, capitalize the first word and every important word in the title.
- Indent the first sentence of the paragraph.
- Introduce the topic of the paragraph in the first sentence.
- Be sure that all sentences in the paragraph deal with the topic.
- Present ideas in the paragraph in logical order.
- In the last sentence make a final statement about the topic.

The following suggestions will help you write more interesting paragraphs.

- Select a topic you know something about.
- Try to begin sentences in different ways.
- Add details to your sentences to make them more interesting.
- Try to avoid overused words, such as *fine, nice,* and *good.*

Practice: If the statement is true, write *yes.* If the statement is not true, write *no.*

_____ 1. The first sentence of a paragraph begins at the left edge of the page.

_____ 2. The topic of the paragraph is introduced in the last sentence.

_____ 3. At least three main topics should be included in a paragraph.

_____ 4. It is important to know something about your topic.

_____ 5. You should try to begin every sentence the same way.

Answers to Guide 28 Practice Exercises

Guide 28a

1. The topic is a new bowling alley.   2. The paragraph describes the alley.

Guide 28b

1. No   2. No   3. No   4. Yes   5. No

Speaking and Listening

Guide 29a | **When you speak in front of a group, follow these guidelines:**

- Speak slowly and clearly enough so that everyone can understand you.
- Make eye contact with the audience.
- Use appropriate language.
- Before you speak, plan the order in which you will say things. When you speak, follow that order.
- Change the volume and tone of your voice to emphasize your main ideas and important points.
- Avoid saying *um.* Try not to use the word *and* too often.
- Finish your talk by repeating your main idea or most important point.

Guide 29b | **When you listen to a speaker or group of speakers, follow these guidelines:**

- Listen carefully and courteously.
- Try to identify a speaker's ideas.
- Take notes if important information is being presented.
- If the speaker is telling about something that happened, pay attention to the order in which events happened.
- If the speaker is describing something, try to picture it in your mind.
- If the speaker is trying to persuade the audience of something, try to determine which statements are facts and which are opinions.
- Be ready to ask questions when the speaker finishes.

Writing Letters
The Friendly Letter

Guide 30a A friendly, or informal, letter has five parts: the heading, the greeting (or salutation), the body, the complimentary close, and the signature.

1. The *heading* tells where and when the letter is written.

2. The *greeting* (or salutation) greets the person to whom the letter is written.

3. The *body* contains the message.

4. The *complimentary close* expresses courtesy or affection.

5. The *signature* is the name of the person writing the letter.

Heading: 3315 Terry Way
                                             Oklahoma City, OK 73119
                                             January 18, 1999

Greeting
(or Salutation):   Dear Thomas,

Body: It was a treat to get your letter. I showed it to my family. Your new job sounds interesting.
                           Guess what? I have a new job, too, selling programs at the soccer games. The pay isn't bad, and I get to see all the games free.
                           If you can come up for spring vacation, I'll plan a get-together with Ahmad and Russ. Write me as soon as you know what your plans are.

Complimentary close: Sincerely,

Signature: Walt

Practice: On these lines list in order the five parts of a friendly letter.

1. _____   4. _____

2. _____   5. _____

3. _____

Guide 30b **Capitalize and punctuate the parts of a friendly letter according to the rules below.**

1. In the heading, capitalize the name of the street, the name of the city, both letters of the postal code abbreviation for the state, and the name of the month. Place a comma between the name of the city and the postal code abbreviation for the state. Place a comma between the day of the month and the year.

> 4076 Marshall Street
> Nashville, TN 37202
> July 14, 1999

2. Capitalize the first word and the name in the greeting. Place a comma after the greeting.

> Dear Aunt Tina,

3. Capitalize the first word of the complimentary close. Place a comma after the close.

> Sincerely yours,

Practice: Rewrite the following heading, greeting, and complimentary close for a friendly letter, using capital letters and punctuation marks correctly.

1. 1609 south first st.

   orlando fl 32802

   august 9 1999

   _____

2. dear mark _____

3. yours truly _____

Answers to Guide 30 Practice Exercises

Guide 30a
1. Heading
2. Greeting (or Salutation)
3. Body
4. Complimentary close
5. Signature

Guide 30b
1. 1609 South First St.
   Orlando, FL 32802
   August 9, 1999
2. Dear Mark,
3. Yours truly,

The Business Letter

Guide 31a	A business letter has the five parts of the friendly letter and a sixth part, the inside address. The inside address gives the name and address of the person or company to whom the letter is written.

Heading:

                                    1421 Central Avenue
                                    Peoria, IL 61601
                                    January 23, 2000

Inside address: Hahn's Hobby Shop
                      1414 Lahoma Avenue
                      Miami, FL 33101

Greeting: Dear People:

Body: In your winter catalogue you advertised a new model car customizing kit, No. 451–j, which was to be ready by the first of this year. Please let me know whether the kit is now available and what it will cost.

Complimentary close: Very truly yours,

Signature: Jerome Becerra

Practice: List in order the six parts of a business letter.

1. _____   4. _____

2. _____   5. _____

3. _____   6. _____

Guide 31b	In a business letter use a formal greeting and complimentary close. The signature should give the full name of the person writing the letter.

        Dear Ms. Blank: (if the letter is addressed to a person)
        Dear Manager: (if the letter is addressed to a company)
        Sincerely yours,
        Very truly yours,
        Yours truly,

Practice: Answer the questions below.

1. What would be the greeting to use in a business letter to a Doctor Williams?_____

_____

2. What would be a greeting to use in a letter to a company? _____

_____

3. Is the full name or only the first name used in the signature of a business letter? _____

_____

Guide 31c Capitalize and punctuate the parts of a business letter according to the rules below.

1. In the heading capitalize the name of the street, the name of the city, both letters of the postal code abbreviation for the state, and the name of the month. Place a comma between the name of the city and the postal code abbreviation for the state. Place a comma between the day of the month and the year.

> 716 Winthrop St.
> Kingston, RI 02881
> April 30, 1998

2. In the inside address capitalize the name of the person or company, the name of the street, the name of the city, and both letters of the postal code abbreviation for the state. Place a period after a title of respect if it is abbreviated and after an initial.

> Ms. Emma Martinelli
> 2815 Harmon Way, Apt. B
> Dover, DE 19901

3. Capitalize the first word of the greeting. Place a colon after the greeting.

> Dear Ms. Martinelli:

4. Capitalize the first word of the complimentary close. Place a comma after the close.

> Sincerely yours,

Practice: Rewrite the following inside address, greeting, and complimentary close for a business letter, using capital letters and punctuation marks correctly.

1. dr susan a franklin _____

   1403 clark st. _____

   terra haute IN 47808 _____

2. dear dr franklin _____

3. very truly yours _____

Answers to Guide 31 Practice Exercises

Guide 31a
1. Heading
3. Greeting
5. Complimentary close

2. Inside address
4. Body
6. Signature

Guide 31b
1. Dear Dr. Williams:
3. The full name is used.

2. Dear Manager:

Guide 31c
1. Dr. Susan A. Franklin
   1403 Clark St.
   Terre Haute, IN 47808
2. Dear Dr. Franklin:
3. Very truly yours,

The Envelope Address

Guide 32 **Follow the rules below in addressing an envelope.**

1. Place the return address (the address of the sender) in the upper left-hand corner of the envelope. Include the correct zip code.

2. Place the name and address of the person or company to whom the letter is addressed in the center of the envelope. Include the correct zip code.

3. In each address capitalize the name of the person, the name of the street, the name of the city, and both letters of the postal code abbreviation for the state. Place a comma between the name of the city and the abbreviation for the state. Here is a listing of the postal code abbreviations for the 50 states, the District of Columbia, and three territories.

Alabama	AL	Kentucky	KY	Ohio	OH
Alaska	AK	Louisiana	LA	Oklahoma	OK
Arizona	AZ	Maine	ME	Oregon	OR
Arkansas	AR	Maryland	MD	Pennsylvania	PA
California	CA	Massachusetts	MA	Puerto Rico	PR
Colorado	CO	Michigan	MI	Rhode Island	RI
Connecticut	CT	Minnesota	MN	South Carolina	SC
Delaware	DE	Mississippi	MS	South Dakota	SD
District of		Missouri	MO	Tennessee	TN
Columbia	DC	Montana	MT	Texas	TX
Florida	FL	Nebraska	NE	Utah	UT
Georgia	GA	Nevada	NV	Vermon	VT
Guam	GU	New Hampshire	NH	Virgin Islands	VI
Hawaii	HI	New Jersey	NJ	Virginia	VA
Idaho	ID	New Mexico	NM	Washington	WA
Illinois	IL	New York	NY	West Virginia	WV
Indiana	IN	North Carolina	NC	Wisconsin	WI
Iowa	IA	North Dakota	ND	Wyoming	WY
Kansas	KS				

Jerome Atkins
1421 Central Ave., Apt. 14
Peoria, IL 61601

Wilson Hobby Shop
1414 Lahoma Avenue
Miami, FL 33101

Practice: Address the envelope below to Mr. Mack Hammond, 1243 Windsor Place, Gainesville, Texas 76240. Use the following return address: Walt Jenkins, 3315 Terry Way, Oklahoma City, Oklahoma 73119.

Answers to Guide 32 Practice Exercises

Walt Jenkins
3315 Terry Way
Oklahoma City, OK 73119

Mr. Mack Hammond
1243 Windsor Place
Gainesville, TX 76240

Troublesome Words and Expressions
Teach and Learn

Guide 33 — The verb *teach* means "to give instruction or to show how something is done." The verb *learn* means "to receive instruction or to find out how to do something."

Mr. Benjamin will *teach* us to dance this year.

My aunt finally *learned* how to speak French.

Practice: Underline the proper word in parentheses.

1. Did your father (teach, learn) you to swim?

2. No, I (taught, learned) to swim at the community pool.

3. This year I want to (teach, learn) how to do the backstroke.

4. I'm going to be (taught, learned) to swim faster in meets.

Answers to Guide 33 Practice Exercises

1. teach   2. learned   3. learn   4. taught

Lie and Lay

Guide 34 — The verb *lie* means "to rest, recline, or remain in one place." The verb *lay* means "to put or place an object on something."

The principal parts of *lie* are *lie, lay,* and *lain.*

> Bingo always *lies* on the rug after dinner.
> This morning Bingo *lay* by the stove without moving.
> Bingo has *lain* on the porch all afternoon.

The principal parts of *lay* are *lay, laid,* and *laid.*

> Please *lay* the place mats on the table.
> Olivia *laid* one place mat beside the vase.
> She had *laid* a tablecloth on the table yesterday.

Practice: Underline the proper word in parentheses.

1. You will feel better if you (lie, lay) down for a while.

2. Be sure to clean your boots before you (lie, lay) them on the shelf.

3. Does your cat like to (lie, lay) in the sun?

4. Let's (lie, lay) these logs beside the grill.

5. When I (lie, lay) down to watch television, I usually fall asleep.

1. lie   2. lay   3. lie   4. lay   5. lie

May and *Can*

Guide 35	Use *may* to ask or give permission to do something. Use *can* to show that someone is able to do something.

> *May* I borrow your umbrella?
>
> I *can* count to ten in German.

Practice: Underline the proper word in parentheses.

1. Ms. Suzuki, (may, can) I leave work early today?

2. Yes, Roger, you (may, can) leave if you have a good reason.

3. (May, Can) you tell me where Howard Street is?

4. Mr. Sanchez said that we (may, can) borrow his car.

1. may   2. may   3. Can   4. may

Sit and *Set*

Guide 36	*Sit* means "to be seated." *Set* means "to place or put."

The principal parts of *sit* are *sit*, *sat*, and *sat*.

> My cousin likes to *sit* in the yard every afternoon.
> This afternoon she *sat* under the big tree.
> She has *sat* there for ten minutes.

The principal parts of *set* are *set*, *set*, and *set*.

> Will you please *set* the table for me?
> Toby *set* the plates on the table an hour ago.
> He had *set* six chairs around the table earlier today.

Practice: Underline the proper word in parentheses.

1. The panting dog (sat, set) down in the middle of the street.

2. I usually (set, sit) my watch on the dresser at night.

3. Why do you (sit, set) there so quietly?

4. She (sat, set) quietly beside the river.

Answers to Guide 36 Practice Exercises

1. sat   2. set   3. sit   4. sat

Doesn't and Don't

Guide 37   *Doesn't is a contraction of does not. Don't is a contraction of do not. Use doesn't when speaking of one person or thing. Use don't when speaking of more than one. Use don't with the pronouns I, we, and you.*

Adele doesn't have a middle name.
The *suits don't* go on sale.
Don't you have any change?

Practice: Underline the proper word in parentheses.

1. The girl (doesn't, don't) have a sister.

2. My cats (doesn't, don't) usually chase birds.

3. She (doesn't, don't) seem to like her job.

4. Enrico (doesn't, don't) want to leave yet.

5. (Doesn't, Don't) you ever jog around the lake?

Answers to Guide 37 Practice Exercises

1. doesn't   2. don't   3. doesn't   4. doesn't   5. Don't

Into and In

Guide 38   Use *into* to refer to movement from the outside to the inside. Use *in* to refer to something already inside.

Mr. Guerrero ran *into* the garage when the fire started.
The hose was *in* the garage.

Practice: Underline the proper word in parentheses.

1. Paul and Mario were driving (in, into) town from the lake.

2. A large bird flew (into, in) the car through an open window.

3. Mario tried to stop, but he drove (into, in) a ditch.

4. The bird flew out of the car window and (into, in) a huge, leafy tree.

5. "No one will ever believe there was a bird (into, in) the car," said Mario.

Answers to Guide 38 Practice Exercises

1. into   2. into   3. into   4. into   · 5. in

Double Negatives

Guide 39 | Words such as *no, not, nobody, none, never,* and *hardly* are negative words. Use only one negative word to express a negative thought.

Laura *hasn't no* hat. (double negative)

Laura *has no* hat. (or) Laura *hasn't* any hat. (correct)

There *isn't hardly* any food left. (double negative)

There is *hardly* any food left. (correct)

Practice: Underline the proper word in parentheses.

1. He couldn't see (nothing, anything) at all.

2. None of the girls (weren't, were) there.

3. Let's not make (any, no) more bracelets today.

4. Haven't you (never, ever) read *Great Expectations*?

5. I (can, can't) hardly hear what you are saying.

Answers to Guide 39 Practice Exercises

1. anything   2. were   3. any   4. ever   5. can

Unnecessary Words

Guide 40 | Omit words that are unnecessary to the meaning of a sentence.

Helen *she* has a new hobby. (unnecessary word)

Helen has a new hobby.

I have *got* a new coat. (unnecessary word)

I have a new coat.

He is in *like* serious trouble. (unnecessary word)

He is in serious trouble.

Where is the dog *at*? (unnecessary word)

Where is the dog?

That *there* car is dirty. (unnecessary word)

That car is dirty.

The box fell off *of* the shelf. (unnecessary word)

The box fell off the shelf.

Where are you going *to*? (unnecessary word)

Where are you going?

The quarterback *went and* scored a touchdown. (unnecessary words)

The quarterback scored a touchdown.

Practice: Draw a line through each unnecessary word in the sentences below.

1. Where is your skateboard at?

2. This here movie is interesting.

3. The girl went and ran into the street.

4. The man drove off of the road.

5. They like walked all the way to the game.

6. Marco he has caught a cold.

7. Naila is like the smartest person!

8. Don't go and lose your ticket.

Answers to Guide 40 Practice Exercises

The following words should be crossed out:
1. at   2. here   3. went, and   4. of
5. like   6. he   7. like   8. go, and

Expressions to Be Avoided

| Guide 41 | In speaking and writing, avoid using expressions that may be inappropriate. |

Use	*Avoid*	*Use*	*Avoid*
am not, is not,		get	git
are not	ain't	grew, grown	growed
ate	et	heard	heered
bought	buyed	himself, themselves	hisself, theirselves
can	kin	knew, known	knowed
could have	could of	must have	must of
dragged	drug	ought not	hadn't ought
drew, drawn	drawed	these flowers, those flowers	them flowers

Practice: Underline the proper word in parentheses.

1. Why (aren't, ain't) you dressed yet?

2. I (should of, should have) called you last night.

3. The dog (drug, dragged) the blanket across the yard.

4. (Them, Those) people down the street are good neighbors.

5. Roberto made this lamp (hisself, himself).

6. Yesterday I (drawed, drew) a picture with charcoal.

Answers to Guide 41 Practice Exercises

1. aren't   4. Those
2. should have   5. himself
3. dragged   6. drew

Using a Dictionary

| Guide 42 | Use a dictionary to find the following information about a word: spelling, pronunciation, syllable division, and meaning. |

Words in a dictionary are arranged in alphabetical order.

The respelling of a word for pronunciation is given after the entry word. The syllable given the most stress is followed by a heavy accent (´). A syllable given somewhat less stress is followed by a light accent mark (´). Study the pronunciation key in the dictionary you use.

lighthouse (līt´hous´)

Practice: List four kinds of information a dictionary gives about a word.

1. _____   3. _____

2. _____   4. _____

Alphabetical Order

| Guide 43a | Words in a dictionary are arranged in alphabetical order: a, b, c, d, e, f, g, h, i, j, k, l, m, n, o, p, q, r, s, t, u, v, w, x, y, z. Words that begin with the same first letter are arranged in alphabetical order according to the second, third, and following letters. |

antelope	fear	janitor	owl	umbrella
ashes	feather	kangaroo	parrot	violin
bell	ginger	lawn	quail	wind
cotton	glass	leopard	radio	winter
dollar	hawk	mason	sailing	xylophone
ear	hobby	milk	sailor	yearling
eye	ice	nest	tiger	yearn
father	icy	opal	tulip	zebra

Practice: Write the words in each group in the order in which they would appear in a dictionary.

1. drive   avenue   street   _____

2. lesson   course   grammar   _____

3. pattern   purple   person   _____

4. melon   minor   market   _____

5. thrust   thrush   throw   _____

6. freight   fruit   fright   _____

Spelling

Guide 43b It is important to spell words correctly when you put ideas into written form. If you are unsure of the spelling of a word, check a dictionary.

after	close	guess	order	thought
always	could	heavy	other	through
anything	country	hundred	people	track
beautiful	different	job	ready	truly
business	early	kept	real	until
center	enough	letter	received	usually
chair	every	many	sold	very
change	family	might	spent	whole
chase	felt	money	start	written
chief	friend	never	state	young

Answers to Guide 43 Practice Exercises

1. avenue, drive, street
2. course, grammar, lesson
3. pattern, person, purple
4. market, melon, minor
5. throw, thrush, thrust
6. freight, fright, fruit

Division of Words

Guide 44a A syllable is a part of a word that is spoken as a unit. Never divide a one-syllable word. When dividing a word at the end of a line, divide it between syllables. Place a hyphen at the end of a syllable and write the rest of the word on the next line.

green (one syllable—do not divide)

pa-per (two syllables)

in-no-cent (three syllables)

Practice: In the list below, underline the words that should not be divided.

1. bridge
2. thirsty
3. three
4. second
5. brown
6. window
7. seven
8. scene
9. hallway
10. elegant
11. thunder
12. grand

Guide 44b | **Follow the rules below in dividing words into syllables.**

1. The sound of the first vowel in a word determines where a two-syllable word should be divided. If the first vowel has a long sound, divide the word after this vowel. If the first vowel has a short sound, divide the word after the consonant following this vowel.

begin	*be-gin*	(*e* has a long sound)
locust	*lo-cust*	(*o* has a long sound)
winter	*win-ter*	(*i* has a short sound)
ugly	*ug-ly*	(*u* has a short sound)

2. If a two-syllable word contains a double consonant, divide the word between the two consonants.

   hammer   *ham-mer*   funny   *fun-ny*

3. When the final consonant of a verb is doubled before *ing* is added, divide the word between the two consonants.

   trim   trimming   *trim-ming*   hit   hitting   *hit-ting*

4. When a verb ends in a double consonant, divide the word before *ing*.

   yell   yelling   *yell-ing*   spill   spilling   *spill-ing*

5. When you are unsure about the division of a word, consult a dictionary.

Practice: Divide the words below into syllables. Place a hyphen between the syllables.

1. detail   _____

2. focus   _____

3. hunter   _____

4. summer   _____

5. willing   _____

6. spelling   _____

7. stepping   _____

8. grabbing   _____

Pronunciation

| Guide 44c | In a dictionary, the sounds of vowels are indicated in the respellings. |

Long Vowel Sound	Short Vowel Sound
date (dāt)	sat (sat)
feel (fēl)	met (met)
like (līk)	pin (pin)
old (ōld)	not (not)
rule (rūl)	hut (hut)

The sounds of the marked vowels are illustrated by key words at the bottom of the dictionary page. Additional vowel sounds are shown by other diacritical markings in a dictionary.

Practice: Use a dictionary to answer the questions below.

1. How is the sound of long *i* shown in the dictionary? _____

2. How is the sound of short *e* shown? _____

3. How is the sound of long *o* shown? _____

4. How is the sound of *a* in *call* shown? _____

5. How is the sound of *u* in *mule* shown? _____

Answers to Guide 44 Practice Exercises

Guide 44a
The following words should be underlined:
1. bridge   3. three   5. brown   8. scene   12. grand

Guide 44b
1. de-tail   5. wil-ling
2. fo-cus   6. spell-ing
3. hun-ter   7. step-ping
4. sum-mer   8. grab-bing

Guide 44c
Answers will correspond to the dictionary used.

Sentence Structure
Subject

Guide 45a	A sentence must have a subject and a predicate. The simple subject is the noun or pronoun that the sentence is about.

The *strawberry* is related to roses.   *I* like strawberries.

Practice: Underline the noun or pronoun that is the simple subject of each sentence below.

1. Strawberries are not really berries.

2. True berries have seeds inside them.

3. A strawberry's "seeds" are on the outside.

4. They are actually individual fruits.

Guide 45b	A simple subject may be compound—that is, made up of two or more nouns or pronouns or a combination of nouns and pronouns joined by a conjunction.

My *sister* and *I* went shoe shopping.

Practice: In the sentences below, underline the nouns or pronouns that make up the compound simple subject.

1. Clogs and sandals were on sale.

2. Flip-flops and wooden clogs were my sister's favorites.

3. She and the clerk discussed the choices.

4. Comfort, style, and price were the main considerations.

Guide 45c	The complete subject is the simple subject and all words that modify it.

Many inches of rain have fallen his year.
Several violent storms have struck the coast.

Practice: Underline the complete subject of each sentence below.

1. A small tornado hit an inland valley.

2. Groups of local citizens organized emergency help.

3. An unexpected, destructive event may bring a community together.

Guide 45d | **The simple predicate is the single verb or verb phrase that expresses the action or state of being of the subject.**

I *learned* mah-jong from my grandmother.

In some sentences the simple predicate is interrupted by other words.

Have you ever *played* this game?

Practice: Underline the simple predicate in each sentence below.

1. Mah-jong is a fascinating game.

2. Players use small tiles instead of cards.

3. They build four walls of tiles.

4. Players collect sets of identical tiles.

5. I have eagerly taught mah-jong to my friends.

6. Will you play this weekend?

Guide 45e | **The simple predicate may be compound, that is, made up of two or more verbs or verb phrases joined by a conjunction.**

Mongooses *kill* and *eat* poisonous snakes.

They *are* not immune to poison but *can fight* snakes safely.

Practice: Underline each verb or verb phrase that makes up the compound predicate in each sentence below.

1. A mongoose dodges and pounces with lightning speed.

2. Mongooses are fierce but can be tamed.

3. People tamed them and brought them from Africa and Asia to places such as Hawaii.

4. The mongooses attacked rodent pests but also harmed native birds.

Guide 45f | The complete predicate is the verb or verb phrase and all other words that are not part of the complete subject.

Many different theories *explain the moon's origin*.

Practice: Underline the complete predicate in each sentence below.

1. The moon might once have been part of the earth.

2. The sun's gravity could have created a bulge on the earth.

3. That bulge might have broken off and formed the moon.

Direct Object

Guide 45g | The direct object is the noun or pronoun that receives the action of a verb.

Renée made a *jacket*.

Practice: Underline the direct objects in the sentences below.

1. She designed it herself.

2. First she cut the cloth.

3. Then she sewed the pieces together.

4. Next year she will attend a school for fashion design.

Guide 45h | Object forms of personal pronouns are used as direct objects.

The producer and director flew *me* to Hollywood.
I thanked *him* and *her*.

Practice: Underline the direct objects in the sentences below.

1. I met them at the movie studio.

2. They considered me for a part in a movie.

3. Later a big star asked them for the part.

4. In the end they picked him for the movie.

Predicate Noun and Predicate Adjective

Guide 45i Predicate nouns and predicate adjectives are part of the complete predicate of a sentence. They follow linking verbs—verbs that show being or a state of being, such as *is, are, was, were, become,* and *seem,* and sometimes *look, feel, smell,* and *taste.*

A predicate noun renames the subject of a sentence.

She is an *artist.*   He became an excellent *sculptor.*

A predicate adjective describes the subject of a sentence.

That painting is *famous.*   The colors look unusually *vibrant.*

Practice: Each sentence has either a predicate noun or a predicate adjective. Draw one line under each predicate noun. Draw two lines under each predicate adjective.

1. Manuela has become a respected painter.

2. Most of her works are landscapes.

3. Her hills look golden.

4. Her trees seem incredibly tall.

Answers to Guide 45 Practice Exercises

Guide 45a
1. Strawberries   2. berries
3. "seeds"   4. They

Guide 45b
1. Clogs, sandals
2. Flip-flops, clogs
3. She, clerk
4. Comfort, style, price

Guide 45c
1. A small tornado
2. Groups of local citizens
3. An unexpected, destructive event

Guide 45d
1. is   3. build   5. have taught
2. use   4. collect   6. will play

Guide 45e
1. dodges, pounces
2. are, can be
3. tamed, brought
4. attacked, harmed

Guide 45f
1. might once have been part of the earth
2. could have created a bulge on the earth
3. might have broken off and formed the moon.

Guide 45g
1. it   2. cloth
3. pieces   4. school

Guide 45h
1. them   2. me
3. them   4. him

Guide 45i
1. painter   2. landscapes
3. golden   4. tall

INDEX OF HANDBOOK

(The numbers refer to Handbook Guide numbers, not page numbers.)

HANDBOOK

Score Chart

LESSON	PERFECT SCORE	MY SCORE	LESSON	PERFECT SCORE	MY SCORE	LESSON	PERFECT SCORE	MY SCORE
1	16		34	44		67	36	
2	33		35	25		68	36	
3	51		36	22		69	22	
4	75		37	21		70	20	
5	25		38	20		71	26	
6	19		39	30		72	43	
7	30		40	12		73	32	
8	38		41	41		74	31	
9	20		42	105		75	99	
11	40		44	28		77	40	
12	6		45	16		78	10	
13	25		46	13		79	10	
14	52		47	56		80	30	
15	45		48	30		81	26	
16	15		49	32		82	52	
17	36		50	38		83	64	
18	10		51	18		84	22	
19	20		52	22		85	29	
20	24		53	111		86	102	
22	52		55	26		88	16	
23	30		56	25		89	27	
24	20		57	28		90	30	
25	10		58	22		91	42	
26	56		59	20		92	57	
27	65		60	20		93	26	
28	37		61	16		94	22	
29	18		62	21		95	26	
30	18		63	30		96	42	
31	36		64	126		97	93	
33	28		66	22		98	96	